CONTENTS

WAYS TO PLAY

LONE QUEST

Playing alone can be a great way to pass the time or to study up so you crush your next bout of bar trivia! As you go through each round in the book, record your answers for the full round on a sheet of paper before checking the answers. Tally up your points for the round and record them in the dedicated pages in the back of this book titled "scoring'. Tally for individual rounds and total up your points for every round. There are 1,230 possible total points.

EVERY ONE FOR THEMSELVES

To get started, gather your friends and choose a host who will read out the questions and answers. One person can be the host for all game play OR you can rotate the host for each round. The host may participate in the round, but keep an eye on 'em so they don't look ahead to the answers. Participants will record their answers for each round on a sheet of paper and points will be tallied for everyone for each round. Consider adding a time limit for each question to keep the game moving.

BRUTAL ELIMINATION

Determine how many elimination rounds you wish to play (recommend 10+) participants sit in a circle and the host reads one question to the person to their left. That person has 45 seconds to correctly answer or they are eliminated. Continue around the circle until there is one person standing. The last person standing receives one point for the round. Continue for as many rounds as you determined when you began. At the end, the person with the most points wins.

TEAMS

Same as for 'Everyone For Themselves' Except that participants are broken out into teams to collaborate on answers.

Enjoyed the challenge? Had a blast with friends and family?
If this trivia game book brought laughter, learning, or a little friendly competition to your day, we'd be thrilled if you shared the love!

Your 5-star review helps others discover the joy—and keeps the trivia coming!

1

LITERATURE

NAME THE WORK

1. — "War is peace, Freedom is Slavery, Ignorance is Strength"

2. — "Happy families are all alike; every unhappy family is unhappy in its own way"

3. — "Whenever you feel like criticizing anyone, just remember that all the people in this world haven't had the advantages that you've had"

4. — "It is a tale told by an idiot, full of sound and fury, signifying nothing"

5. — "The world is indeed full of peril, and in it there are many dark places; but still there is much that is fair, and though in all lands love is now mingled with grief, it grows perhaps greater"

6. — "I took a deep breath and listened to the old brag of my heart: I am, I am, I am"

7. — "It's no use going back to yesterday because I was a different person then"

8. — "The Woods are lovely, dark and deep. But I have promises to keep, and miles to go before I sleep"

9. — "The world breaks everyone, and afterward, some are strong at the broken places"

10. — "Life is to be lived, not controlled, and humanity is won by continuing to play in the face of certain defeat"

11. — "I am no bird; and no net ensnares me: I am a free human being with an independent will, which I now exert to leave you"

12. — "There must be something in books, something we can't imagine, to make a woman stay in a burning house; there must be something there. You don't stay for nothing"

13. — "I have always depended on the kindness of strangers"

14. — "It is a truth universally acknowledged, that a single man in possession of a good fortune, must be in want of a wife"

15. — "I learned to recognise the thorough and primitive duality of man; I saw that of the two natures that contended in the field of my consciousness, even if I could rightfully be said to be either, it was only because I was radically both"

DID YOU KNOW ...

Bram Stoker's "Dracula" was inspired by the historical figure Vlad III, also known as Vlad the Impaler. While Vlad was not a vampire, his cruel methods of punishing enemies influenced the character of Count Dracula.

ANSWERS
1. 1984-George Orwell 2. Anna Karenina-Leo Tolstoy 3. The Great Gatsby-F. Scott Fitzgerald
4. Macbeth-William Shakespeare 5. The Fellowship of the Ring-J.R.R. Tolkien
6. The Bell Jar- Sylvia Plath 7. Alice's Adventures in Wonderland-Lewis Caroll
8. Stopping by the Woods on a Snowy Evening-Robert Frost 9. A Farewell to Arms-Ernest Hemingway
10. Invisible Man-Ralph Ellison 11.   Jane Eyre-Charlotte Brontë
12. Fahrenheit 451-Ray Bradbury 13. A Streetcar Named Desire-Tennessee Williams
14. Pride and Prejudice-Jane Austen 15. Strange Case of Dr. Jekyll and Mr. Hyde-Robert Louis Stevenson

NAME THE STORY

1. — This short story was first published in 1841, features the fictional detective C. Auguste Dupin, and is considered the first modern detective story

2. — A young girl named Liesel steals books and shares them with her neighbors during World War II in this novel narrated by Death

3. — A physician is marooned on a deserted island for nearly three decades, where he must learn to survive and adapt to his solitary existence

4. — This novel features the characters Mole, Badger, Ratty and Mr. Toad who has a passion for motorcars and gets into trouble with the law

5. — This novella features the character of a well-respected scientist that, as the result of an experiment undergoes a transformation that brings forth his darker side

6. — This tale features the character Ichabod Crane and his encounter with the ghostly figure known as the Headless Horseman

7. — This novel follows the life of a young girl named Anne Shirley, an imaginative orphan who is mistakenly sent to live with Marilla and Matthew Cuthbert

8. — Set in post-World War I, this novel explores the disillusionment and trauma experienced by a group of expatriates living in Paris

9. — This classic novel follows the story of an orphan named Pip and his encounters with the mysterious benefactor who funds his education

10. — A collection about a housemaid with a knack for causing confusion by interpreting instructions in a literal way, such as dressing a chicken in clothes or drawing the curtains with a pencil

11. — In this story the main character meets a magical Grasshopper, Ladybug, Centipede, Earthworm, Spider, and Glowworm

12. — In this dystopian novel, Offred recounts her life as a Handmaid in the theocratic Republic of Gilead, where women's roles are strictly defined

13. — This novel follows the story of a shipwrecked sailor who encounters a strange island and its inhabitants, including the enigmatic Prospero

14. — This Gothic novel tells the story of Heathcliff and Catherine Earnshaw, whose passionate but destructive love unfolds on the Yorkshire moors

15. — An ancient Greek epic recounting the adventures of Odysseus as he tries to return home after the Trojan War

DID YOU KNOW ...

Mark Twain, the author of "The Adventures of Tom Sawyer" and "Adventures of Huckleberry Finn," chose his pen name based on his experience as a riverboat pilot. "Mark twain" is a riverboat term meaning the water is two fathoms (12 feet) deep, indicating safe navigation.

ANSWERS
1. The Murders in the Rue Morgue-Edgar Allen Poe 2. The Book Thief-Markus Zusak
3. Robinson Crusoe-Daniel Defoe 4. The Wind in the Willows-Kenneth Grahame
5. Strange Case of Dr. Jekyll and Mr. Hyde-Robert Louis Stevenson
6. The Legend of Sleepy Hollow-Washington Irving 7. Anne of Green Gables-Lucy Maud Montgomery
8. The Sun Also Rises-Ernest Hemingway 9. Great Expectations-Charles Dickens
10. Amelia Bedelia-Peggy Parish 11. James and the Giant Peach-Roald Dahl
12. The Handmaid's Tale-Margaret Atwood 13. The Tempest-William Shakespeare
14. Wuthering Heights-Emily Brontë 15. The Odyssey-Homer

NAME THE AUTHOR

1. — Who wrote the science fiction novel "Dune"?

2. — Who wrote the novel "One Hundred Years of Solitude"?

3. — Who wrote "The Divine Comedy," an epic poem widely considered a masterpiece of world literature?

4. — Who wrote Middle Earth's "There and Back Again"?

5. — Who wrote the novel "Do Androids Dream of Electric Sheep?" which inspired the film "Blade Runner"?

6. — Who wrote the novel "Fight Club," which was later adapted into a film directed by David Fincher?

7. — Which Irish author wrote "Ulysses," a modernist novel that takes place over a single day in Dublin and is considered a literary masterpiece?

8. — Who wrote the fictional book "Hogwarts: A History," a reference guide mentioned throughout the "Harry Potter" series?

9. — Who wrote the The Call of Cthulhu, published in 1928?

10. — Which French writer is known for his adventure novels, including "Twenty Thousand Leagues Under the Sea" and "Journey to the Center of the Earth"?

11. — Which English author created the iconic character Mary Poppins in a series of children's books?

12. — Who is the author of "The Hitchhiker's Guide to the Galaxy," a humorous science fiction series that originated as a radio comedy?

13. — Which American author wrote "The Color Purple," a novel that addresses issues of race, gender, and the power of resilience in the face of adversity?

14. — In the dystopian society of "Fahrenheit 451," who is the author of the forbidden book "The Bible," which plays a central role in the novel's plot?

15. — Who wrote the fictional play "The Mousetrap," a central element in the murder mystery "The Murder of Roger Ackroyd" by Agatha Christie?

DID YOU KNOW ...

Ernest Hemingway once bet that he could write a complete story in just six words. He wrote: "For sale: baby shoes, never worn." This concise tale is a powerful example of his ability to convey deep emotions with minimal words.

ANSWERS
1. Frank Herbert 2. Gabriel García Márquez 3. Dante Alighieri 4. Bilbo Baggins 5. Philip K. Dick
6. Chuck Palahniuk 7. James Joyce 8. Bathilda Bagshot 9. H.P. Lovecraft 10. Jules Verne
11. P.L. Travers 12. Douglas Adams 13. Alice Walker
14. God (In the context of the novel, the authorship of the Bible is attributed to God)
15. W. Shakespeare (as adapted in the novel)

GRAB BAG

1. — What author coined "The three laws of robotics"?

2. — In this narrative style, the story is presented as a series of letters, diary entries, or documents, providing a firsthand account of events. What is this form called?

3. — What is the title of the first book in Stieg Larsson's "Millennium" series?

4. — What prestigious literary award is given annually for a distinguished work of fiction by an American author?

5. — Who is known as the "Queen of Crime" and authored detective novels like "Murder on the Orient Express"?

6. — What literary term refers to the repetition of the same consonant sounds at the beginning of words?

7. — What is the full title of the novel by Stephen King that was adapted into the film "The Shawshank Redemption"?

8. — What literary award is presented annually by the Mystery Writers of America for the best in mystery fiction?

9. — Which novel by Aldous Huxley explores a futuristic world where conformity is maintained through the use of drugs?

10.— What Russian novel explores the moral and philosophical dilemmas faced by Prince Myshkin?

11.— This narrative style involves telling a story through the eyes of an all-knowing narrator who has access to the thoughts and feelings of all characters. What is this form called?

12.— In which poem does T.S. Eliot write, "April is the cruelest month"?

13.— Which Tom Wolfe book explores the cultural and social scene of New York City in the 1980s and coined the term "Masters of the Universe" for powerful financial professionals?

14.— Which U.S. state serves as the setting for many of Jon Grisham's legal thrillers, including "A Time to Kill" and "The Client"?

15.— This narrative form involves telling a story backward, starting with the conclusion and then revealing events that lead up to it. What is this storytelling technique called?

DID YOU KNOW ...

In 1926, Agatha Christie, the Queen of Crime, went missing for 11 days. The circumstances surrounding her disappearance remain unclear, and to this day, it is a mystery that has never been fully solved. She was later found at a spa hotel, claiming amnesia.

ANSWERS
1. Isaac Isimov 2. Epistolary 3. The Girl With the Dragon Tattoo 4. The Pulitzer Prize for Fiction
5. Agatha Christie 6. Alliteration 7. Rita Hayworth and Shawshank Redemption
8. Edgar Allan Poe Award (Edgar Award) 9. Brave New World 10. "The Idiot" by Fyodor Dostoevsky
11. Omniscient Narration 12. The Waste Land 13. The Bonfire of the Vanities 14. Mississippi
15. Reverse Chronology

CHILDREN'S STORIES

1. — What is the name of Pippi Longstocking's house?

2. — What literary award is given annually for an outstanding work of children's literature?

3. — What is the name of the young orphan who befriends a bear in A.A. Milne's stories?

4. — What children's book features a character named Max who sails to the land of the Wild Things?

5. — What is the name of the magical land that Mary discovers when she plants magical flower seeds in Frances Hodgson Burnett's novel?

6. — In the "Magic Tree House" series, what are the names of the siblings who discover the magical tree house?

7. — What is the title of the first book in the "Little House" series by Laura Ingalls Wilder?

8. — Who wrote the classic children's book "The Tale of Peter Rabbit"?

9. — What is the title of the first book in the "Nancy Drew" mystery series?

10. — Who wrote the "Ramona" series, which follows the adventures of a mischievous girl named Ramona Quimby?

11. — What is the name of the young pig in E.B. White's "Charlotte's Web"?

12. — What classic children's book tells the story of a young boy's journey to the North Pole on a magical train?

13. — What is the title of the first book in the "His Dark Materials" trilogy by Philip Pullman?

14. — What classic children's book features a family of anthropomorphic bears, including Papa Bear, Mama Bear, and Brother Bear?

15. — What classic children's book features a big red dog?

DID YOU KNOW ...

A.A. Milne's beloved "Winnie-the-Pooh" series was initially titled "Edward Bear." The change came about when Milne's son, Christopher Robin, renamed his teddy bear Winnie after a Canadian black bear at the London Zoo named Winnipeg. The name stuck, and the stories became timeless classics.

ANSWERS
1. Villa Villekula 2. The Newbery Medal 3. Christopher Robin
4. Where the Wild Things Are by Maurice Sendak 5. The Secret Garden 6. Jack and Annie
7. Little House in the Big Woods 8. Beatrix Potter 9. The Secret of the Old Clock by Carolyn Keene
10. Beverly Cleary 11. Wilbur 12. The Polar Express 13. The Golden Compass
14. The Berenstain Bears series 15. Clifford the Big Red Dog

GRAB BAG 2

1. — What was the first novel written by Jane Austen?

2. — What French novelist, known for works like "Les Misérables" and "The Hunchback of Notre-Dame," is considered a key figure of the Romantic movement?

3. — What literary device involves the repetition of vowel sounds within nearby words in a line of poetry?

4. — What 17th-century English poet and politician wrote the epic poem "Paradise Lost," exploring the Fall of Man?

5. — What influential 16th-century work, written by Niccolò Machiavelli, explores political power and strategy?

6. — What is the name of the ship that Herman Melville's "Moby-Dick" is centered around?

7. — What is the name of the fictional detective created by Sir Arthur Conan Doyle?

8. — Who authored the Pulitzer Prize-winning novel "All the Light We Cannot See"?

9. — What literary term refers to the use of words that imitate the sounds associated with the objects or actions they refer to?

10.— Who is considered the "Father of English Literature" and authored "The Canterbury Tales"?

11.— What is the highest literary award given for a single work in the English language, awarded annually by the Swedish Academy?

12.— What is the title of the first book in the "A Series of Unfortunate Events" by Lemony Snicket?

13.— What is the literary device where a word or phrase is repeated at the beginning of consecutive clauses or sentences?

14.— Who wrote the novel "Crime and Punishment," exploring the psychological and moral dilemmas of the main character, Raskolnikov?

15.— What literary technique involves giving human-like qualities to non-human entities or abstractions?

DID YOU KNOW ...

The longest novel ever written is "Artamène ou le Grand Cyrus," an epic work written by French author Madeleine de Scudéry. Published between 1649 and 1653, it consists of approximately 13,095 pages and over 2 million words.

ANSWERS
1. "Sense and Sensibility" 2. Victor Hugo 3. Assonance 4. John Milton 5. "The Prince" 6. Pequod
7. Sherlock Holmes 8. Anthony Doerr 9. Onomatopoeia 10. Geoffrey Chaucer
11. The Nobel Prize in Literature 12. "The Bad Beginning" 13. Anaphora 14. Fyodor Dostoevsky
15. Personification

21st CENTURY AUTHORS

1. — Which American author wrote the Pulitzer Prize-winning novel "The Road," published in 2006?

2. — Who wrote the dystopian trilogy "The Hunger Games," with the first book published in 2008?

3. — Who wrote the critically acclaimed novel "The Goldfinch," published in 2013?

4. — Which British author is known for the "His Dark Materials" trilogy?

5. — Who authored "The Book Thief," a novel narrated by Death and set during World War II?

6. — Which Norwegian author penned the highly acclaimed novel "A Man Called Ove," a heartwarming story about an elderly curmudgeon?

7. — Who wrote the best-selling novel "The Help," set in the early 1960s during the Civil Rights Movement?

8. — Which American author is known for the series "A Series of Unfortunate Events" and "All the Wrong Questions"?

9. — What Canadian author wrote the novel "Life of Pi"?

10.— Name the Indian-American author of "The Namesake" and "Interpreter of Maladies"

11.— Name the author of "The Ocean at the End of the Lane" and "American Gods"

12.— Which American author is famous for the "Outlander" series?

13.— Name the British author of the "Cormoran Strike" detective series, writing under the pseudonym Robert Galbraith

14.— Who wrote the science fiction novel "The Martian," which later became a successful film?

15.— Which American author wrote the Pulitzer Prize-winning novel "The Brief Wondrous Life of Oscar Wao"?

DID YOU KNOW ...

Mark Z. Danielewski, known for his novel "House of Leaves," continued to push the boundaries of literature with "The Familiar" series. Released in multiple volumes, the series incorporates unconventional formatting, various fonts, and even color changes to enhance the storytelling experience.

ANSWERS
1. Cormac McCarthy 2. Suzanne Collins 3. Donna Tartt 4. Philip Pullman 5. Markus Zusak
6. Fredrik Backman 7. Kathryn Stockett 8. Lemony Snicket (Daniel Handler) 9. Yann Martel
10. Jhumpa Lahiri 11. Neil Gaiman 12. Diana Gabaldon 13. J.K. Rowling 14. Andy Taylor Weir
15. Junot Díaz

2

SPORTS

ACHIEVEMENTS

1. — Name the only NFL team to record a perfect season resulting in a Super Bowl victory

2. — Who holds the record for the most career touchdown receptions in the NFL?

3. — Which golfer holds the record for the most Masters Tournament victories?

4. — Who holds the world record for the fastest 100 meters in track and field, with an astonishing time of 9.58 seconds set at the 2009 World Championships in Berlin?

5. — What Boxer holds the record for the most career wins?

6. — Who has won the most Grand Slam singles titles in women's tennis?

7. — Who holds the record for the most career points in the NBA?

8. — Who holds the record for the most goals scored in a single NHL season?

9. — Which baseball player holds the record for the most career home runs?

10.— Who is the most decorated Olympian of all time?

11.— Who holds the record for the most Grand Slam singles titles in men's tennis?

12.— Who has won the FIFA World Player of the Year the most times?

13.— Who is the all-time leader in career passing completions in the NFL?

14.— What female alpine Skier has the most World Cup Wins?

15.— Who holds the record for the most rushing yards in a single NFL season?

DID YOU KNOW ...

Joe DiMaggio holds the record for the most consecutive games with a hit in Major League Baseball (MLB). In 1941, the New York Yankees outfielder achieved hits in 56 consecutive games, a record that still stands.

ANSWERS
1. Miami Dolphins (1972) **2.** Jerry Rice **3.** Jack Nicklaus **4.** Usain Bolt **5.** Len Wickwar **6.** Margaret Court
7. LeBron James **8.** Wayne Gretzky **9.** Barry Bonds **10.** Michael Phelps **11.** Novak Djokovic
12. Lionel Messi **13.** Tom Brady **14.** Mikaela Shiffrin **15.** Eric Dickerson

NAME THE ATHLETE

1. — Who won the first ever Tour de France?

2. — Which NBA player holds the record for most points scored in a single game?

3. — Who is the only boxer to win titles in eight different weight classes?

4. — Which athlete is known as the "Flying Tomato"?

5. — What NFL player holds the record for the most 4th quarter comebacks in a single season?

6. — Who is the only goalkeeper to have won the FIFA World Player of the Year?

7. — Who are the only two players to have recorded 30 interceptions and 30 sacks in their NFL career?

8. — Who holds the record for the most consecutive wins in professional boxing, with an undefeated streak of 50-0?

9. — Who is the first and only female gymnast to win three consecutive World All-Around titles?

10.— What MMA fighter earned the nickname "The Arm Collector" with their use of their Armbar, often leading to quick victories?

11.— Which NBA player holds the record for the most triple-doubles in a career?

12.— Who is the only male tennis player to have completed the Golden Slam (winning all four Grand Slam titles and Olympic gold in a calendar year)?

13.— Which NFL player has the most 1,000 yard rushing seasons?

14.— Who is the only driver to have won the Indianapolis 500, Daytona 500, and the Formula One World Championship?

15.— Which Brazilian soccer legend is known as "The King" and scored over 1,000 career goals?

DID YOU KNOW ...

In 2020, David Ayres, a Zamboni driver for the Toronto Maple Leafs, made NHL history by stepping in as an emergency backup goalie for the Carolina Hurricanes. Ayres went on to play in the game against the Leafs, becoming the oldest goaltender to win his NHL debut.

ANSWERS
1. Maurice Garin 2. Wilt Chamberlain 3. Manny Pacquiao 4. Shaun White 5. Kirk Cousins
6. Nadine Angerer 7. Ray Lewis and Rodney Harrison 8. Floyd Mayweather Jr. 9. Simone Biles
10. Ronda Rousey 11. Russell Westbrook 12. Andre Agassi 13. Emmitt Smith 14. Mario Andretti 15. Pelé

COLLEGE SPORTS

1. ___ Which men's college basketball program has the most NCAA Division I tournament championships?

2. ___ Which college is home to the "Golden Gophers" in their athletic programs?

3. ___ Which school has won the most Division I College World Series?

4. ___ Which women's volleyball program has won the most Division I national championships?

5. ___ Who was the first freshman to win the Naismith Award?

6. ___ Who is the only player to win the Heisman Trophy twice?

7. ___ Which school has had the most NCAA tournament appearances in men's basketball?

8. ___ In college football, which Division I school has the longest winning streak in NCAA history?

9. ___ Who has the most career points in NCAA men's basketball?

10.— In college baseball, which school has the longest winning streak in NCAA history?

11.— In women's college basketball, which program has the most NCAA championships?

12.— Who is the only Haisman Trophy winner to play in the NBA?

13.— Who are the only two quarterbacks to win an NCAA National Championship and a Super Bowl?

14.— Which college women's softball program has won the most Division I championships?

15.— Which men's college basketball program has had the most Naismith winners?

DID YOU KNOW ...

The Stanford Tree, the unofficial mascot of Stanford University, originated in 1975 when a member of the Stanford Band decided to dress up as a tree during a football game halftime show. Despite not being an official mascot, the Stanford Tree has become an iconic symbol of the university.

ANSWERS
1. UCLA 2. University of Minnesota 3. USC 4. Stanford 5. Kevin Durant 6. Archie Griffin
7. University of Kentucky 8. University of Oklahoma 9. Pete Marovich 10. University of Texas
11. University of Connecticut 12. Charlie Ward 13. Joe Montana and Joe Namath 14. UCLA 15. Duke

GRAB BAG

1. — In golf, what is the term for a score of one stroke under par on a hole?

2. — Which city hosted the first modern Olympic games?

3. — What is the diameter of a standard basketball hoop in inches?

4. — Which country won the first FIFA World Cup in 1930?

5. — Who was the first woman to climb Mount Everest?

6. — What is the maximum number of players a soccer team can have on the field at once during a match?

7. — Which country won the first Rugby World Cup?

8. — In what year did the first modern Winter Olympic Games take place?

9. — What is the length of an Olympic swimming pool in meters?

10.— What is the maximum number of clubs a golfer is allowed to have in their bag during a round?

11.— In what year did the NFL officially merge with the AFL?

12.— What country has the most gold medals in Olympic Wrestling?

13.— In which year were the first official rules of basketball published by James Naismith?

14.— In what year did the first recorded game of rugby take place?

15.— Which country won the first ever Women's World Cup in soccer?

DID YOU KNOW ...

Chess boxing is a hybrid sport that combines chess and boxing. Competitors alternate between rounds of chess and boxing, requiring both mental strategy and physical prowess. The World Chess Boxing Organization (WCBO) oversees and regulates official matches.

ANSWERS
1. Birdie 2. Athens, Greece 3. 18 inches 4. Uruguay 5. Jinko Tabei 6. 11 7. New Zealand 8. 1924
9. 50 meters 10. 14 11. 1970 12. Soviet Union 13. 1892 14. 1823 15. United States

GRAB BAG 2

1. — What is the last tennis major tournament in a calendar year?

2. — What MLB team has retired the most jersey numbers?

3. — What company is the main sponsor of the PGA playoffs?

4. — Cassius Marcellus Clay, Jr. was the original name of what famous athlete?

5. — Founded in 1873, what is the oldest team in the Canadian Football League?

6. — What color is the middle ring in the symbol of the Olympic Games?

7. — In terms of a soccer box score, what does "FT" stand for?

8. — In what sport is a "ringer" scored when the heel calks clear the stake?

9. — How many innings must an MLB game reach before it's an "official game"?

10.— What is the only 2-word MLB team name without an "x" in it?

11.— Who is the only player in NBA history to win 6 regular season Most Valuable Player awards?

12.— What is the longest event, in meters, of a decathlon?

13.— What baseball position is scored number 8?

14.— What jersey number was the first to be retired by any team in MLB?

15.— Just before moving into Dodger Stadium in 1962, what stadium did the Los Angeles Dodgers call home?

DID YOU KNOW ...

The longest recorded drive in professional golf history was hit by Mike Austin during the U.S. National Seniors Open Championship in 1974. His drive, which was aided by a strong wind, traveled an incredible 515 yards (471 meters).

ANSWERS
1. US Open 2. New York Yankees 3. FedEx 4. Mohammed Ali 5. Toronto Argonauts 6. Black 7. Full Time
8. Horseshoes 9. 5 10. Blue Jays 11. Kareem Abdul-Jabbar 12. 1500m 13. Center Field
14. 4 (Lou Gehrig) 15. (Los Angeles) Memorial Coliseum

GRAB BAG 3

1. ___ Of the NBA's teams, which team has the longest tenured head coach?

2. ___ What was the nickname of the 1991 Michigan's recruiting class that included Jalen Rose?

3. ___ What is the name of the golf event held every 2 years between the US and an International team representing the rest of the world minus Europe?

4. ___ What is the official ball weight in ounces for a standard Major League Baseball?

5. ___ In yards, how long is an NFL end zone?

6. ___ What was the only NFL team that John Madden coached in his career?

7. ___ Who was the first woman to lead a lap in the Indianapolis 500?

8. ___ Jon Gruden won a Super Bowl in his first year as head coach of what team?

9. ___ What MLB stadium was originally opened in 1996 as Centennial Olympic Stadium?

10.— In which city did the first recorded game of baseball take place?

11.— What is the diameter of a standard golf hole in inches?

12.— In tennis, what is the term for a score of zero?

13.— How many players are on the field for each team in a standard game of field hockey?

14.— Which Grand Slam tennis tournament is played on a clay court?

15.— What is the term for a score of one stroke over par on a golf hole?

DID YOU KNOW ...

The marathon distance of 26.2 miles (42.195 kilometers) was standardized during the 1908 London Olympics. The distance was extended so that the race could start at Windsor Castle and finish in front of the royal box at the Olympic Stadium.

ANSWERS
1. San Antonio Spurs 2. Fab Five 3. Presidents Cup 4. 5 ounces 5. 10 yards 6. Raiders 7. Danica Patrick
8. Tampa Bay Buccaneers 9. Turner Field 10. Hoboken, New Jersey 11.4.25 inches 12. Love 13. 11
14. The French Open 15. Bogey

GRAB BAG 4

1. — Who did Muhammad Ali defeat in 1974's Rumble in the Jungle?

2. — In 1954, Roger Bannister became the first athlete to run 1 mile in under how many minutes?

3. — In seconds, how long is the shot clock in NCAA basketball?

4. — Every Grey Cup championship game has been played in what country?

5. — How many total schools make the NCAA Division 1 Men's Basketball Championship tournament?

6. — Name all 4 NHL team names that do NOT end with an "S"

7. — What school hosts the First Four of the NCAA Division 1 Men's Basketball Championship tournament?

8. — Of the 6 teams that Randy Johnson pitched for in his MLB career, which did he appear in the most games with?

9. — What is the highest number an NFL quarterback can wear on their jersey?

10.— Who received a reported $25 million for a 1995 boxing match that lasted 89 seconds?

11.— What word did Tampa Bay's MLB franchise drop from their name in 2007?

12.— What company currently owns the naming rights to the Superdome?

13.— What is the term for when a baseball pitcher executes an illegal move?

14.— What NBA head coach has won 3 NBA titles in a row 3 different times?

15.— What is the maximum number of strikes a bowler can bowl in a single game?

DID YOU KNOW ...

The longest tennis match in history took place at Wimbledon in 2010 between John Isner and Nicolas Mahut. The match lasted for 11 hours and 5 minutes over three days, with Isner eventually winning 6–4, 3–6, 6–7(7), 7–6(3), 70–68.

ANSWERS
1. George Foreman 2. 4 3. 30 seconds 4. Canada 5. 68 6. Avalanche, Lightning, Kraken and Wild
7. University of Dayton 8. Mariners 9. 19 10. Mike Tyson 11. Devil 12. Caesars Entertainment 13. Balk
14. Phil Jackson 15. 12

3

MOVIES & TV

MOVIE LINES

1. — "Hasta la vista, baby"

2. — "They've done studies, you know. 60 percent of the time, it works every time"

3. — "You mean you'll put down your rock and I'll put down my sword, and we'll try and kill each other like civilized people?"

4. — "Why did it have to be snakes?"

5. — "Florals? For Spring? Groundbreaking"

6. — "364 days until next year's hockey tryouts, I have to toughen up"

7. — "Fish are friends not food"

8. — "It's 106 miles to Chicago, we got a full tank of gas, half a pack of cigarettes, it's dark, and we're wearing sunglasses"

9. — "If You're A Bird, I'm A Bird"

10. — "Ohana means family, and family means nobody gets left behind or forgotten"

11. — "They may take our lives, but they'll never take our freedom!"

12. — "The only skater to win four national championships and an adult film award"

13. — "Exercise gives you endorphins. Endorphins make you happy. Happy people just don't shoot their husbands, they just don't"

14. — "Listen, you promise me something, OK? Just if you're ever in trouble, don't be brave. You just run, OK? Just run away"

15. — "Fasten your seatbelts. It's going to be a bumpy night"

DID YOU KNOW ...

One of the most famous lines in cinematic history, from the film "Casablanca" (1942), was not originally in the script. Humphrey Bogart, who played Rick Blaine, improvised the line during filming.

ANSWERS
1. Terminator 2: Judgment Day (1991) **2.** Anchorman: The Legend of Ron Burgundy (2004)
3. The Princess Bride (1987) **4.** Raiders of the Lost Ark (1981) **5.** The Devil Wears Prada (2006)
6. Happy Gilmore (1996) **7.** Finding Nemo (2003) **8.** The Blues Brothers (1980) **9.** The Notebook (2004)
10. Lilo & Stitch (2002) **11.** Braveheart (1995) **12.** Blades of Glory (2007) **13.** Legally Blonde (2001)
14. Forest Gump (1994) **15.** All About Eve (1950)

MOVIE LINES 2

ROUND RULES: In this round, the question will include a famous movie line. The answer will be the name of the movie.

-OR-

Two points can be awarded per question. One point naming the movie and one for naming the year the movie was released.

1. — "By my deeds I honor him, V8"

2. — "Be goooooooooooood"

3. — "Would you like to put some clothes on?" "Oh, would you like to pick the outfit that you break up with me in?"

4. — "From now on you will speak only when spoken to, and the first and last word out of your filthy sewers will be 'sir'"

5. — "Marry Me, June"

6. — "It's like a stew, right? Why do they call it that? If you're gonna name a food, you should give it a name that sounds delicious"

7. — "If you vote for me, it will be summer all year round"

8. — "What kind of host invites you to his house for the weekend and dies on you?"

9. — "You gotta hand it to the old girl. I never saw nobody buffalo Bill the way she buffaloed Bill"

10. — "But for now, for your customer's sake, for your daughter's sake, ya might wanna think about buying a quality product from me"

11. — "I'm your density. I mean... destiny"

12. — "See the way she did that? Sugar Ray could do that. The girl's got Sugar!"

13. — "There are only 2 rules. You can't tell anybody you're God, believe me you don't want that kind of attention, and you can't mess with free will"

14. — "Now, I can sell the star-crossed lovers from District 12"

15. — "True love is hard to find. Sometimes you think you have true love and then you catch the early flight home from San Diego and a couple of nude people jump outta your bathroom, blindfolded like a magic show"

DID YOU KNOW ...

"There's a snake in my boot!": This memorable line from "Toy Story" (1995) was originally suggested by Tom Hanks, the voice of Woody. It became one of the most quotable lines from the film.

ANSWERS
1. Mad Max: Fury Road (2015) 2. E.T. (1982) 3. Forgetting Sarah Marshall (2008)
4. Full Metal Jacket (1987) 5. Walk the Line (2005) 6. Ratatouille (2007) 7. Napoleon Dynamite (2004)
8. Weekend at Bernie's (1989) 9. Kill Bill, Vol. 2 (2004) 10. Tommy Boy (1995)
11. Back to the Future (1985) 12. Million Dollar Baby (2004) 13. Bruce Almighty (2003)
14. The Hunger Games (2012) 15. Old School (2003)

MOVIE MONSTERS

1. — What classic horror film features a town terrorized by a giant, radioactive arachnid?

2. — What creature does Van Helsing pursue in the 1931 film directed by Tod Browning?

3. — In this 1954 Japanese film, what monstrous creature emerges from the sea and attacks Tokyo?

4. — Who is the fictional character with razor-sharp fingers and the ability to haunt and kill teenagers in their dreams?

5. — What film features a family who encounters a group of cannibalistic mutants in the New Mexico desert?

6. — In this animated film, monsters generate power by scaring children

7. — In this film, a widowed mother, Amelia, and her troubled son, Samuel, become haunted by a sinister presence from a mysterious pop-up book

8. — Who appears every 27 years to prey on the fear of children?

9. — What classic horror movie features a character named Norman Bates who runs a secluded motel?

10.— In this 2018 film, a mother must protect her family from blind creatures that hunt by sound

11.— What classic horror movie features a creature brought to life using electricity in a laboratory?

12.— What 1982 movie features a shape-shifting alien in an antarctic research station?

13.— What 1979 film features a character named Ellen Ripley battling a deadly extraterrestrial species?

14.— In this 1999 found-footage horror film, a group of students investigate strange occurrences in Maryland

15.— What Guillermo del Toro film features a character named Pale Man, a grotesque creature with eyes in the palms of its hands?

DID YOU KNOW ...

The marketing for "The Blair Witch Project" (1999) deliberately maintained the illusion that the events in the film were real. The actors' disappearance was even reported on missing persons databases, contributing to the film's found-footage authenticity.

ANSWERS
1. Tarantula (1955) 2. Dracula (1931) 3. Godzilla 4. Freddie Kreuger 5. The Hills Have Eyes (1977)
6. Monsters, Inc. (2001) 7. The Babadook (2014) 8. Pennywise - It 9. Psycho (1960)
10. A Quiet Place (2018) 11. Frankenstein (1931) 12. The Thing (1982) 13. Alien (1979)
14. The Blair Witch Project (1999) 15. Pan's Labyrinth (2006)

ACADEMY AWARDS

1. — Who is the iconic gold statuette named after, awarded annually by the Academy of Motion Picture Arts and Sciences?

2. — Which film won the Best Picture award at the 92nd Academy Awards in 2020?

3. — What film is the only sequel ever to win the Oscar for Best Picture?

4. — Which film won the first-ever Best Picture award at the Oscars?

5. — Who is the only actor to receive an Oscar nomination for acting in a Lord of the Rings film for Fellowship of the Ring in 2001?

6. — Which film won the first Oscar for Best Animated Feature in 2002?

7. — Which actress holds the record for the most nominations in the acting categories?

8. — What is the only X-rated film to win the Best Picture Oscar?

9. — In what year were the first Academy Awards held?

10.— Who is the only actor to have won an Oscar and has two parents that have also won an Oscar?

11.— Who was the first woman to win the Academy Award for Best Director for "The Hurt Locker" (2009)?

12.— After a four hour and twenty three minute ceremony in 2002, a rule was introduced limited speeches to how many seconds?

13.— What individual has received the most Oscars?

14.— Who holds the record for the most wins in the Best Director category at the Oscars with 4 wins for "The Informer" (1935), "The Grapes of Wrath" (1940), "How Green Was My Valley" (1941), and "The Quiet Man" (1952).

15.— What film won the first Oscar for Best Makeup in 1982?

DID YOU KNOW ...

Tatum O'Neal is the youngest person ever to win a competitive Oscar. She was only 10 years old when she won the Best Supporting Actress award for "Paper Moon" in 1974. On the other hand, the oldest Oscar winner is Christopher Plummer, who won Best Supporting Actor for "Beginners" at the age of 82 in 2012.

ANSWERS
1. Bette Davis' first husband, Harmon Oscar Nelson 2. Parasite 3. "The Godfather Part II" (1974) 4. "Wings" (1927) 5. Ian McKellen 6. Shrek 7. Meryl Streep 8. "Midnight Cowboy" (1969). 9. 1929 10. Liza Minnelli 11. Kathryn Bigelow 12. 45 seconds 13. Walt Disney 14. John Ford 15. An American Werewolf in London

TV

1. — What was Ashton Kutcher's version of Candid Camera?

2. — What was the name of the tallest and oldest Teletubbie?

3. — What sitcom features a diner named Monk's Café?

4. — Boy Meets World was set in the suburb of what city?

5. — The "Hellmouth' was a supernatural portal on what TV Show?

6. — What Spike TV show is hosted by food and beverage consultant, Jon Taffler?

7. — What TV show features a US president named Fitzgerald Grant?

8. — On Friday Night Lights, what is the mascot for East Dillon High School?

9. — What Nickelodeon title character was known as the "Boy Genius"?

10.— What was the name of the Tanner family dog on Full House?

11.— What cast member has appeared in the most episodes of Saturday Night Live?

12.— On House of Cards, what state does Frank Underwood represent in congress?

13.— What was the name of the first spinoff of Law & Order?

14.— In what TV show does the main character speak these words in it's opening lines: "To all law enforcement entities, this is not an admission of guilt. I am speaking to my family now"?

15.— What is the first word of the Cheers theme song?

DID YOU KNOW ...

Cartoon Network, the popular cable channel dedicated to animated programming, was almost named "Luna-Toon" during its development. However, the name was changed to Cartoon Network shortly before its launch in 1992, reflecting its focus on cartoons and animation.

ANSWERS
1. Punk'd 2. Tinky Winky 3. Seinfeld 4. Philadelphia 5. Buffy the Vampire Slayer 6. Bar Rescue
7. Scandal 8. Lions. 9. Jimmy Neutron 10. Comet 11. Kenan Thompson 12. South Carolina
13. Law & Order Special Victim's Unit (SVU) 14. Breaking Bad 15. Making

TV 2

1. — On King of the Hill, what is the name of Bobby's middle school?

2. — What show popularized the acronym "GTL"?

3. — What was Walker from Walker, Texas Ranger's first name?

4. — What SNL alum starred in Just Shoot Me, 8 Simple Rules, and Rules of Engagement?

5. — What TV show featured a character named Sookie St. James?

6. — "It's a Sunshine Day" is a song related to what TV show?

7. — On Orange is the New Black, what state was Piper Chapman born in?

8. — Charmed was set in what California city?

9. — On Spongebob Squarepants, although Gary's a snail, what animal's sound does he make?

10.— What show featured a coffee shop named The Talon and a school newspaper named The Torch?

11.— What was Tiffany Amber-Thiessen's character name in Beverly Hills, 90210?

12.— What TV show got a Lego makeover for its 550th episode, titled 'Brick Like Me'?

13.— Who was the host of MTV's America's Best Dance Crew?

14.— What supernatural drama on The CW is based on the popular book series of the same name written by L.J. Smith?

15.— What was Will Schuester's final job title on the show Glee?

DID YOU KNOW ...

The first television remote control, called the "Lazy Bones," was developed by Zenith Radio Corporation in 1950. It was connected to the TV set by a wire and used sound waves to change channels. However, it was not very popular due to its limited range and the fact that it required batteries for the sound mechanism.

ANSWERS
1. Tom Landry 2. Jersey Shore 3. Cordell 4. David Spade 5. Gilmore Girls 6. The Brady Bunch
7. Connecticut 8. San Francisco 9. Cat 10. Smallville. 11. Valerie 12. The Simpsons 13. Mario Lopez
14. The Vampire Diaries 15. Principal

GRAB BAG

1. __ What was the first feature-length animated movie ever released?

2. __ Who won the Academy Award for Best Actress for her role in the 2017 film "La La Land"?

3. __ In the TV series "Stranger Things," what is the name of the parallel dimension?

4. __ In which film does Tom Hanks play a character stranded on a deserted island with a volleyball named Wilson?

5. __ Who directed the 1991 film "The Silence of the Lambs"?

6. __ Which actor portrayed James Bond in the films "License to Kill" and "The Living Daylights"?

7. __ What was the first cable television network to broadcast 24 hours a day?

8. __ What is the name of the device that enables time travel in the DeLorean in the "Back to the Future" film series?

9. __ In the TV series "Friends," what is Ross Geller's profession?

10.— Who won the Academy Award for Best Supporting Actress for her role in the 2016 film "Fences"?

11.— What is the name of the character played by Tom Cruise in the "Mission: Impossible" film series?

12.— What is the name of the pub where the main characters frequently gather in the TV series "How I Met Your Mother"?

13.— Who won the Academy Award for Best Director for the 2018 film "The Shape of Water"?

14.— In the TV series "Game of Thrones," what is the name of Jon Snow's direwolf?

15.— Who won the Academy Award for Best Supporting Actor for his role in the 2013 film "Dallas Buyers Club"?

DID YOU KNOW ...

The classic film "Back to the Future" (1985) was initially titled "Spaceman From Pluto" according to a memo from Universal Pictures' Sid Sheinberg. However, director Robert Zemeckis and producer Steven Spielberg successfully persuaded Sheinberg to drop the title.

ANSWERS
1. Snow White and the Seven Dwarfs (1937) 2. Emma Stone 3. The Upside Down 4. Cast Away
5. Jonathan Demme 6. Timothy Dalton 7. CNN 8. Flux Capacitor 9. Paleontologist 10. Viola Davis
11. Ethan Hunt 12. MacLaren's 13. Guillermo del Toro 14. Ghost 15. Jared Leto

4

MUSIC

GRAB BAG

1. — What was the first music video ever played on MTV when it launched in 1981?

2. — Who was the first woman to be inducted into the Rock and Roll Hall of Fame?

3. — In what year did The Beatles make their debut on The Ed Sullivan Show?

4. — What famous music venue in San Francisco was a focal point for the counterculture music scene in the 1960s?

5. — In what year did Michael Jackson release his best-selling album, "Thriller"?

6. — In what year was the first Grammy's ceremony held?

7. — Who composed the famous "Four Seasons" concertos?

8. — Which musician was known as the "High Priestess of Soul"?

9. — What famous composer was deaf for much of his life but continued to compose music?

10.— In what year did Elvis Presley release his first studio album?

11.— Which iconic jazz trumpeter was nicknamed "Satchmo" and was a key figure in the development of jazz music?

12.— Who composed the famous ballet scores "Swan Lake," "The Nutcracker," and "The Sleeping Beauty"?

13.— What singer-songwriter, known for hits like "Fire and Rain" and "You've Got a Friend," emerged from the 1970s folk rock scene?

14.— What American rapper and actor rose to fame with albums like "Doggystyle" and "The Chronic" in the 1990s?

15.— What American singer, known as the "King of Swing," was a prominent bandleader during the Swing Era?

DID YOU KNOW ...

The first known recording of a human voice predates Thomas Edison's invention of the phonograph. In 1860, French inventor Édouard-Léon Scott de Martinville created a device called the phonautograph, which could capture sound waves on paper. Although he never intended to play back the recordings, modern technology has allowed us to convert his recordings into playable sound, making them the earliest known recordings of the human voice.

ANSWERS
1. "Video Killed the Radio Star" by The Buggles 2. Aretha Franklin 3. 1964 4. Fillmore Auditorium 5. 1982
6. 1959 7. Antonio Vivaldi 8. Nina Simone 9. Ludwig van Beethoven 10. 1956 11. Louis Armstrong
12. Pyotr Ilyich Tchaikovsky 13. James Taylor 14. Snoop Dogg 15. Benny Goodman

NAME THE ARTIST

1. — "Do I wanna Know?," "505," "Brainstorm"

2. — "Don't Blink," "There Goes My Life," "The Boys of Fall"

3. — "Crazy in Love," "Halo," "Formation"

4. — "Fallin'," "No One," "Girl on Fire"

5. — "People are Strange," "Alabama Song," "Roadhouse Blues"

6. — "Purple Haze," "Hey Joe," "All Along the Watchtower"

7. — "If U Can't Dance," "Say You'll Be There," "2 Become 1"

8. — "Seven Nation Army," "Icky Thump," "Fell in Love with a Girl"

9. — "Viva la Vida," "Fix You," "The Scientist"

10. — "My Heart Will Go On," "The Power of Love," "It's All Coming Back to Me Now"

11. — "All of Me," "Ordinary People," "Love Me Now"

12. — "Ain't No Sunshine," "Lean on Me," "Lovely Day"

13. — "Girls Just Want to Have Fun," "Time After Time," "True Colors"

14. — "Blinding Lights," "Can't Feel My Face," "Starboy"

15. — "The Man," "Shake It Off," "Blank Space"

DID YOU KNOW ...

The legendary Queen frontman Freddie Mercury had four extra teeth in the back of his mouth, contributing to his distinctive vocal sound. Mercury chose not to have them removed because he believed they helped him achieve a wider vocal range.

ANSWERS
1. Arctic Monkeys 2. Kenny Chesney 3. Beyonce 4. Alicia Keys 5. The Doors 6. Jimi Hendrix 7. Spice Girls 8. The White Stripes 9. Coldplay 10. Celine Dion 11. John Legend 12. Bill Withers 13. Cyndi Lauper 14. The Weeknd 15. Taylor Swift

NAME THE ARTIST 2

1. — "Any Man of Mine," "You're Still the One," "When You Kiss Me"

2. — "Soul Meets Body," "We Looked Like Giants," "Here to Forever"

3. — "She Will Be Loved," "This Love," "Misery"

4. — "The House That Built Me," "Gunpowder & Lead," "Hell On Heels"

5. — "Just A Girl," "Don't Speak," "Hella Good"

6. — "Gimme All Your Lovin'," "Rough Boy," "Tush"

7. — "Do You Believe In Life After Love?," "Believe," "If I Could Turn Back Time"

8. — "Beauty And A Beat," "Needle," "Everybody"

9. — "All Eyez On Me," "California Love," "Life Goes On"

10. — "That's The Way Love Goes," "All For You," "Scream"

11. — "Under The Bridge," "Scar Tissue," "Can't Stop"

12. — "Again," "Are You Gonna Go My Way," "Fly Away"

13. — "Blue Ain't Your Color," "One Too Many," "Somebody Like You"

14. — "Numb," "What I've Done," "In the End"

15. — "Save Me," "Need a Favor," "Son of a Sinner"

DID YOU KNOW ...

Before becoming a rock icon, Jimi Hendrix served in the United States Army as a paratrooper in the 101st Airborne Division. He was honorably discharged in 1962 after injuring himself during a parachute jump.

ANSWERS
1. Shania Twain 2. Death Cab for Cutie 3. Maroon 5 4. Miranda Lambert 5. No Doubt 6. ZZ Top 7. Cher 8. Nicki Minaj 9. Tupac 10. Janet Jackson 11. Red Hot Chili Peppers 12. Lenny Kravitz 13. Keith Urban 14. Lincoln Park 15. Jelly Roll

GRAB BAG 2

1. — What musical term indicates a gradual increase in volume?

2. — What is the name of the first commercial video cassette recorder introduced by Sony in 1975?

3. — Which legendary guitarist, known for his blues style, was nicknamed the "King of the Blues"?

4. — Who is the youngest person to ever win a Grammy?

5. — Which country is the origin of the traditional musical instrument called the didgeridoo?

6. — Which legendary singer is known as the "Queen of Jazz" and won 13 Grammy Awards, including a Lifetime Achievement Award?

7. — Which classical composer is famous for his "Ride of the Valkyries" and "The Ring of the Nibelung" opera cycle?

8. — What is the term for a musical composition that features a solo instrument accompanied by an orchestra?

9. — In what year did the music streaming service Spotify launch?

10.— In what year did Beyoncé release her visual album "Lemonade"?

11.— Who is known for the song "Shape of You" and the album "÷" (Divide)?

12.— Who is the only artist to have won Album of the Year three times in a row (1971, 1972, 1973)?

13.— What is the term for a rapid alternation between two adjacent notes, typically a semitone or whole tone apart?

14.— Who is known as the "King of Country" and has hits like "Amarillo by Morning" and "Check Yes or No"?

15.— In what year did Whitney Houston release her version of the song "I Will Always Love You"?

DID YOU KNOW ...

Led Zeppelin's members made a secret pact to disband the group if any one of them quit. This pact was made early in their career as a commitment to the unique chemistry and camaraderie they shared.

ANSWERS
1. Crescendo 2. Betamax 3. B.B. King 4. LeAnn Rimes 5. Australia 6. Ella Fitzgerald 7. Richard Wagner 8. Concerto 9. 2008 10. 2016 11. Ed Sheeran 12. Stevie Wonder 13. Trill 14. George Strait 15. 1992

MUSICAL ACHIEVEMENTS

1. __ Who holds the record for the most Grammy Awards won by a female artist?

2. __ Which artist or group holds the record for the most number-one hits on the Billboard Hot 100?

3. __ Which iconic rock band won Album of the Year at the 2017 Grammy Awards for their album "A Moon Shaped Pool"?

4. __ Which song holds the record for the longest time at number one on the Billboard Hot 100?

5. __ Which artist holds the record for the most consecutive number-one hits on the Billboard Hot 100?

6. __ Which American rapper won the Pulitzer Prize for Music in 2018?

7. __ Who holds the record for most "Album of the Year" wins?

8. __ Who holds the record for the most cumulative weeks at number one on the Billboard Hot 100?

9. __ Who is the youngest artist to win Album of the Year at the Grammy Awards?

10. — Who is the youngest artist to have a number-one hit on the Billboard Hot 100?

11. — Which iconic singer-songwriter won the Grammy Award for Album of the Year in 1971 for "Bridge over Troubled Water"?

12. — Who holds the record for the most weeks at number one on the Billboard Hot 100 chart for a solo artist?

13. — Who won the Grammy Award for Best Pop Vocal Album in 2019 for "Sweetener"?

14. — Which artist won Album of the Year at the 2018 Grammy Awards for "24K Magic"?

15. — Which artist holds the record for the most Grammy Awards won in a single night?

DID YOU KNOW ...

The term "diva" originally referred to a female opera singer of outstanding talent. It comes from the Italian word for "goddess." Over time, the term has expanded to encompass female singers of exceptional skill and talent in various genres, particularly pop and R&B.

ANSWERS
1. Beyoncé 2. The Beatles 3. Radiohead 4. Lil Nas X's "Old Town Road" 5. Whitney Houston
6. Kendrick Lamar 7. Taylor Swift 8. Mariah Carey 9. Billie Eilish 10. (Little) Stevie Wonder
11. Simon & Garfunkel 12. Mariah Carey 13. Ariana Grande 14. Bruno Mars 15. Michael Jackson

MOVIE MUSIC

1. — What is the name of the fictional band in the movie "Almost Famous"?

2. — In the movie "A Clockwork Orange," what classical piece is prominently featured?

3. — In "Forrest Gump," what song does Forrest start running to across the country?

4. — What is the title of the song playing when Tom Cruise dances in his underwear in "Risky Business"?

5. — What song does Zoe Deschanel sing in the shower in "Elf"?

6. — In "Wayne's World," the characters sing along to which Queen song in the car?

7. — What song does Heath Ledger's character sing on the bleachers in "10 Things I Hate About You"?

8. — What is the title of the song that plays during the closing credits of "Fight Club"?

9. — What song by The Bee Gees is played during the dance competition scene in "Saturday Night Fever"?

10.— What song does Mike Tyson sing along to in the Hangover?

11.— What song do the Deetzes and their dinner guests involuntarily dance to in Beetlejuice?

12.— This song is the background of Liv Tyler and Ben Affleck's romance in Armageddon

13.— In Reservoir Dogs, before cutting off his hostage's ear, Mr. White takes his time finding the radio station where this song is playing

14.— Patrick Bateman queues up this song before taking an axe to Paul Allen in American Psycho

15.— Josie and her two best friends wore cat ears in this movie rock band

DID YOU KNOW ...

Ray Parker Jr.'s iconic theme song for the film "Ghostbusters" (1984) was originally meant to be a different tune. Parker was asked to come up with a theme song for the movie, but he misinterpreted the request and wrote "Ghostbusters" in just a few days. The song became a massive hit and earned Parker a Grammy Award nomination.

ANSWERS
1. Stillwater 2. Beethoven's Ninth Symphony (Ode to Joy) 3. "Running on Empty" by Jackson Browne
4. "Old Time Rock and Roll" by Bob Seger 5. Baby, It's Cold Outside 6."Bohemian Rhapsody"
7. "Can't Take My Eyes Off You" by Frankie Valli 8. "Where Is My Mind?" by Pixies
9."More Than a Woman" 10. "In the Air Tonight" - Phil Collins
11. Day-O (Banana Boat Song)" by Harry Belafonte 12. "I Don't Wanna Miss A Thing" by Aerosmith
13. "Stuck in the Middle with You" by Stealers Wheel 14. "Hip to be square" - Huey Lewis and the News
15. Josie and the Pussy Cats

FIRST #1 ON BILLBOARD HOT 100

1. — 50 Cent

2. — Wham!

3. — Lady Gaga

4. — Justin Timberlake

5. — Adele

6. — Marvin Gaye

7. — Jennifer Lopez

8. — Elvis Presley

9. — Paula Abdul

10.— Taylor Swift

11.— Katy Perry

12.— Michael Jackson

13.— Usher

14.— Madonna

15.— Rihanna

DID YOU KNOW ...

In 2021, at the age of 95, Tony Bennett became the oldest living artist to achieve a number-one album on the Billboard 200 chart with "Cheek to Cheek," a collaborative album with Lady Gaga. This achievement further cemented Bennett's legendary status in the music industry.

ANSWERS
1. In Da Club **2.** Wake Me Up Before You Go-Go **3.** Just Dance **4.** SexyBack **5.** Rolling in the Deep
6. I Heard It Through the Grapevine **7.** If You Had My Love **8.** I Forgot To Remember To Forget
9. Straight Up **10.** We Are Never Ever Getting Back Together **11.** I Kissed a Girl **12.** Ben **13.** Nice & Slow
14. Like a Virgin **15.** SOS

5

GEOGRAPHY

WORLD CAPITALS

1. — What is the capital of Indonesia?

2. — What is the capital of Thailand?

3. — What is the capital of the Philippines?

4. — What is the capital city of Australia?

5. — Which city is the Southern most capital in the world?

6. — What is the capital of Venezuela?

7. — This Capital city is known for its European-style architecture and is often referred to as the "Paris of South America"

8. — What is the capital of Peru?

9. — What is the capital of Turkey?

10.— Which city serves as the capital of Egypt?

11.— What is the capital of India?

12.— This capital city literally means "Northern Capital" in Mandarin

13.— What is the capital of Canada?

14.— Which city is the capital of South Korea?

15.— What capital city was originally a Roman city called "Lutetia"?

DID YOU KNOW ...

Reykjavik, the capital of Iceland, is known for its use of geothermal energy. The city is powered primarily by renewable energy sources, including geothermal heating, making it one of the greenest capitals in the world.

ANSWERS
1. Jakarta 2. Bangkok 3. Manila 4. Canberra 5. Wellington, New Zealand 6. Caracas
7. Buenos Aires, Argentina 8. Lima 9. Ankara 10. Cairo 11. New Delhi 12. Beijing 13. Ottawa 14. Seoul
15. Paris, France

WATER

1. — Which ocean is the smallest by surface area?

2. — Which sea is bordered by Italy, Croatia, and Greece?

3. — Lake Baikal is the deepest lake in the world. In which country is it situated?

4. — What is the name of the river that flows through Paris?

5. — Which sea is bordered by Cyprus, Syria, and Turkey?

6. — Lake Titicaca, the highest navigable lake in the world, is situated between which two South American countries?

7. — What body of water is bordered by Iraq, Iran, and Kuwait?

8. — Which sea is the largest inland body of water in the world?

9. — Lake Geneva, one of the largest lakes in Western Europe, is shared by which two countries?

10.— The Mississippi River is a major river in North America. In which state does it have its source?

11.— The Amazon River flows through multiple countries in South America. Which ocean does it ultimately empty into?

12.— What is the second-longest river in Europe, flowing through ten countries?

13.— The Strait of Gibraltar connects the Mediterranean Sea to which other body of water?

14.— What is the largest island in the Mediterranean Sea?

15.— The Dead Sea, known for its high salt concentration, is bordered by which two countries?

DID YOU KNOW ...

Bermeja was believed to be an island off the coast of the Yucatán Peninsula, appearing on maps for centuries. However, in the 20th century, extensive searches failed to find it. Today, its existence is disputed, and the mystery of Bermeja remains unsolved, adding an intriguing element to geographical lore.

ANSWERS
1. Arctic Ocean 2. Adriatic Sea 3. Russia 4. Seine River 5. Mediterranean Sea 6. Peru and Bolivia
7. Persian Gulf 8. Caspian Sea 9. Switzerland and France 10. Minnesota 11. The Atlantic Ocean
12. Danube River 13. Atlantic Ocean 14. Sicily 15. Israel and Jordan

NAME THE COUNTRY

1. — Located in Southeast Asia, this country is known as the "Land of Smiles" and is renowned for its vibrant street food and rich cultural heritage

2. — This country is famous for its tulip fields, windmills, and wooden clogs

3. — Which country is known as the "Land of Fire and Ice"?

4. — Which African country is known as the "Pearl of Africa"?

5. — Which two countries share the Iberian Peninsula?

6. — Which country is known as the "Land of a Thousand Hills"?

7. — Which country is known as the "Land of the Midnight Sun"?

8. — Which country, located in South America, is the largest Spanish-speaking country in the world by land area?

9. — This island nation in the Indian Ocean is famous for its diverse wildlife, including lemurs, and is often called the "Eighth Continent"

10.— Which country is known as the "Land of the Rising Sun"?

11.— Which country is known as the "Land of a Thousand Lakes"?

12.— Which African country is often referred to as the "Rainbow Nation" due to its diverse population and post-apartheid policies of reconciliation?

13.— This country, located in the Middle East, is home to Petra, an ancient city carved into rose-red cliffs

14.— Which Asian country is made up of over 7,000 islands and is known for its beautiful beaches, volcanoes, and diverse marine life?

15.— This Southeast Asian country is famous for its ancient temples, including Angkor Wat, and is known as the "Kingdom of Wonder"

DID YOU KNOW ...

Bhutan is known for prioritizing the well-being of its citizens over economic growth. The country measures its success by Gross National Happiness (GNH) rather than Gross Domestic Product (GDP), making it the only country in the world to do so. GNH takes into account factors such as psychological well-being, health, education, and environmental diversity.

ANSWERS
1. Thailand 2. The Netherlands 3. Iceland 4. Uganda 5. Spain and Portugal 6. Rwanda 7. Norway
8. Mexico 9. Madagascar 10. Japan 11. Finland 12. South Africa 13. Jordan 14. Philippines
15. Cambodia

GRAB BAG

1. — Which mountain range is the longest in the world?

2. — Which African city, often referred to as the "Mother City," is known for landmarks like Table Mountain and Robben Island?

3. — What sea, in the North Atlantic Ocean, is distinctive for its seaweed, Sargassum, and is the only sea without a land boundary?

4. — In which ocean would you find the Mariana Trench, the deepest part of the world's oceans?

5. — Which mountain range separates Europe and Asia?

6. — What is the largest island nation in the world?

7. — In which country would you find the city of Casablanca?

8. — Which island nation is known as the "Pearl of the Indian Ocean"?

9. — What is the capital city of Hungary?

10. — Which river flows through the Grand Canyon?

11. — In what U.S. state would you find Denali, the highest peak in North America?

12. — What is the largest desert in the world by area?

13. — Which South American country shares its borders with ten other countries and is the most populous nation on the continent?

14. — In geography, what term is used to describe a narrow, navigable route of water connecting two larger bodies of water?

15. — What is the term for the area in the ocean where sunlight cannot penetrate, and photosynthesis is not possible?

DID YOU KNOW ...

Bir Tawil is a strip of land between Egypt and Sudan that is unclaimed by either country. The border dispute between the two nations has left this area without formal recognition, making it one of the few unclaimed territories in the world.

ANSWERS
1. Andes 2. Cape Town, South Africa 3. Sargassso Sea 4. The Pacific Ocean 5. The Ural Mountains
6. Indonesia 7.Morocco 8. Sri Lanka 9. Budapest 10. Colorado River 11. Alaska 12. Antarctica
13. Brazil 14. Strait 15. Aphotic Zone

GRAB BAG 2

1. ___ What is the term for the study of maps and mapmaking?

2. ___ In which country would you find the iconic Christ the Redeemer statue overlooking the city of Rio de Janeiro?

3. ___ In which European country would you find the region of Transylvania?

4. ___ Which Great Lake is the only one located entirely within the United States?

5. ___ What is the highest mountain in the contiguous United States?

6. ___ Which desert, located in Asia, is the largest cold desert in the world?

7. ___ What is the name of the active volcano located in Italy, famous for its eruption in 79 AD that buried the city of Pompeii?

8. ___ In geography, what term refers to a narrow strip of land connecting two larger landmasses and surrounded by water on two sides?

9. ___ Which strait separates Europe and Asia, connecting the Black Sea to the Mediterranean Sea?

10.— What is the tallest waterfall in the world, located in Venezuela's Canaima National Park?

11.— Which imaginary line, located at 23.5 degrees south of the Equator, marks the southernmost point where the Sun appears directly overhead?

12.— In which U.S. state would you find the Grand Teton National Park?

13.— In which country would you find the ancient city of Troy, famous for the Trojan War in Greek mythology?

14.— Which mountain range forms a natural border between France and Spain?

15.— In which country would you find the city of Timbuktu?

DID YOU KNOW ...

Lesotho, a small country entirely landlocked by South Africa, is known as the "Kingdom in the Sky" because of its high-altitude terrain. It is the only country in the world entirely above 1,000 meters (3,281 feet) in elevation.

ANSWERS
1. Cartography 2. Brazil 3. Romania 4. Lake Michigan 5. Mount Whitney 6.The Gobi Desert
7. Mount Vesuvius 8. Isthmus 9. The Bosporus Strait 10. Angel Falls 11. Tropic of Capricorn 12. Wyoming
13. Turkey 14. The Pyrenees 15. Mali

GRAB BAG 3

1. — What is the capital city of Norway?

2. — Which mountain range runs along the western edge of South America, from Venezuela to Chile?

3. — In geography, what term refers to the distance north or south of the equator, measured in degrees?

4. — What mountain range passes through Morocco, Algeria, and Tunisia?

5. — What is the largest island in the Caribbean Sea?

6. — In which U.S. state is Mount Rushmore, featuring the carved faces of four U.S. presidents?

7. — In geography, what term refers to the science and art of determining the position and elevation of points on the Earth's surface?

8. — In which African country is Mount Kilimanjaro, the highest peak on the continent?

9. — What is the capital city of South Sudan, the youngest country in the world?

10. — Which ocean is the smallest and least deep of the world's five major oceans?

11. — What mountain range spans Czech Republic, Hungary, Poland, Romania, Serbia, Slovak Republic, and Ukraine?

12. — In which U.S. state is the Great Salt Lake located?

13. — In geography, what term refers to the distance east or west of the Prime Meridian, measured in degrees?

14. — What is the capital city of Finland?

15. — In which ocean is the island nation of Maldives located?

DID YOU KNOW ...

The Great Green Wall is an African-led initiative aimed at combating desertification, land degradation, and climate change by creating a mosaic of green and productive landscapes across the Sahel region. The goal is to plant a wall of trees spanning over 7,000 kilometers (4,300 miles) across the continent from Senegal to Djibouti.

ANSWERS
1. Oslo 2. The Andes Mountains 3. Latitude 4. The Atlas Mountains 5. Cuba 6. South Dakota 7. Surveying
8. Tanzania 9. Juba 10. The Arctic Ocean 11. The Carpathian Mountains 12. Utah 13. Longitude
14. Helsinki 15. Indian Ocean

GRAB BAG 4

1. — What is the largest island in the world?

2. — Which African country is the most populous?

3. — In which ocean would you find the Great Barrier Reef, the world's largest coral reef system?

4. — In Geography, what is the term for a group or chain of islands?

5. — Which river flows through Budapest, the capital of Hungary?

6. — Which US state is known as the "Land of 10,000 Lakes"?

7. — Which is the largest province by land area in Canada?

8. — What is the capital city of Poland?

9. — In which African country would you find the Maasai Mara National Reserve, known for its wildlife and annual migration of wildebeest?

10.— Which river is the second-longest in the world and flows through several African countries, including Congo and Angola?

11.— Which river is the longest in Asia and third-longest in the world?

12.— In which African country would you find the ancient city of Carthage?

13.— In which country is the ancient city of Persepolis, known for its historical significance and archaeological remains?

14.— Which valley in Arizona is famous for its red rock formations, including Cathedral Rock and Bell Rock?

15.— What is the term for the point on the Earth's surface directly above the initial rupture or focus of an earthquake?

DID YOU KNOW ...

Mount Everest, the world's highest peak, is still growing. Due to tectonic activity, it is estimated to be rising at a rate of about 4 millimeters (0.16 inches) per year.

ANSWERS
1. Greenland 2. Nigeria 3.The Pacific Ocean (Coral Sea) 4. Archipelago 5. Danube River 6. Minnesota
7. Quebec 8. Warsaw 9. Kenya 10. The Congo River 11. The Yangtze River 12. Tunisia 13. Iran
14. Sedona Valley 15. Epicenter

6

SCIENCE

SCIENTIFIC DISCOVERIES AND THEORIES

ROUND RULES: In this round, the question describes a scientific discovery or theory. The answer is the scientist that is credited for the discovery or theory.

1. — Laws of Motion and Universal Gravitation

2. — Theory of Relativity (E=mc²)

3. — Discovery of radium and polonium, pioneering research on radioactivity

4. — Theory of Evolution by Natural Selection

5. — Theoretical physics and black hole radiation

6. — Germ theory of disease, pasteurization

7. — Big Bang Theory

8. — Heliocentric Theory (model that places the Sun at the center of the universe, with the Earth and other planets revolving around it)

9. — Discovery of penicillin

10.— Laws of inheritance, founding modern genetics

11.— X-ray diffraction work and Photo 51 leading to the discovery of the DNA double helix

12.— Oxygen theory of combustion

13.— Laws of electromagnetic induction and electrolysis

14.— Principle of Buoyancy

15.— The expansion of the universe

DID YOU KNOW ...

Michael Faraday, a pioneering scientist in the fields of electromagnetism and electrochemistry, had little formal education. Despite not attending university, he made significant contributions to science, including the discovery of electromagnetic induction and the laws of electrolysis.

ANSWERS
1. Isaac Newton 2. Albert Einstein 3. Marie and Pierre Curie 4. Charles Darwin 5. Stephen Hawking
6. Louis Pasteur 7. Georges Lemaître 8. Nicholas Copernicus 9. Alexander Fleming 10. Gregor Mendel
11. Rosalind Franklin 12. Antoine Lavoisier 13. Michael Faraday 14. Archimedes 15. Edwin Hubble

SPACE

1. — What is the name of the closest galaxy to the Milky Way?

2. — What is the name of the process by which a star transforms hydrogen into helium, releasing a tremendous amount of energy in the process?

3. — What is the only planet in our solar system that rotates clockwise?

4. — What is the name of the first artificial satellite, launched by the Soviet Union in 1957?

5. — What Apollo 13 astronaut uttered the famous words "Houston, we've had a problem" during the mission's critical situation in space?

6. — Who is known as the "father of modern observational astronomy"?

7. — On what planet is the largest volcano in our solar system, Olympus Mons, located?

8. — What is the name of the spacecraft that carried the first humans to the Moon in 1969?

9. — What is the name of the second-largest dwarf planet in our solar system?

10.— Who was the first human to travel into space?

11.— What is the term for the darkest part of a shadow during a lunar eclipse?

12.— Which spacecraft, launched by NASA in 1977, has traveled the farthest from Earth and is now in interstellar space?

13.— What is the name of the largest moon in our solar system?

14.— Which planet in our solar system has the longest day, lasting approximately 243 Earth days?

15.— What is the point of no return around a black hole, beyond which nothing, not even light, can escape?

DID YOU KNOW ...

Jupiter's Great Red Spot, a massive storm, has been raging for at least 350 years and possibly much longer. It is so large that it could fit three Earths within its boundaries.

ANSWERS
1. Andromeda 2. Nuclear fusion 3. Venus 4. Sputnik 1 5. Jack Swigert 6. Galileo Galilei 7.Mars
8. Apollo 11 9. Eris 10. Yuri Gagarin 11. Umbra 12. Voyager 1 13. Ganymede 14. Venus
15. Event Horizon

BIOLOGY

1. — In genetics, what is the term for the specific location of a gene on a chromosome?

2. — What is the smallest bone in the human body?

3. — What process do cells undergo to divide and produce new cells?

4. — What is the largest cell occurring in the human body? It is just visible to the naked eye and is about the size of a grain of sand

5. — What is the medical term for the collarbone?

6. — What is the longest bone in the human body?

7. — What is the term for the study of viruses and viral diseases?

8. — In molecular biology, what is the term for a change in the sequence of DNA that can be inherited?

9. — What is the scientific name for the human skull?

10.— What part of the cell is responsible for protein synthesis?

11.— What is the name of the small, almond-shaped structure in the brain associated with emotional responses, particularly fear?

12.— What is the term for the process by which the brain modifies its structure and function in response to experience or injury?

13.— Which part of a plant is responsible for the production of sugar through photosynthesis and is often referred to as the "kitchen" of the plant?

14.— Which gas do plants absorb during photosynthesis?

15.— What is the study of the interactions between organisms and their environment?

DID YOU KNOW ...

In 2009, scientists discovered a gene called DEC2 that regulates the amount of sleep a person needs. People with a mutation in this gene, known as the "short sleep" gene, can function well on significantly less sleep than the average person without experiencing adverse effects.

ANSWERS
1. Locus 2. Stapes (found in the middle ear) 3.Mitosis 4. Egg (ovum) 5. Clavicle 6. Femur 7.Virology
8. Mutation 9. Cranium 10. Ribosomes 11. Amygdala 12. Neuroplasticity 13. Leaf
14. Carbon dioxide (CO2) 15. Ecology

GRAB BAG

1. — What is the speed of light in a vacuum? (in kilometers/second)

2. — In physics, what is the unit of measurement for electrical resistance?

3. — What is the process by which a substance transitions directly from a solid to a gas?

4. — What is the process by which plants release water vapor into the atmosphere?

5. — What is the chemical formula for table salt?

6. — In the electromagnetic spectrum, which type of radiation has the shortest wavelength?

7. — What is the speed of sound in air at sea level? (in meters/second)

8. — What is the term for a plant's male reproductive organ, which produces pollen?

9. — Which part of the human brain is responsible for regulating basic bodily functions like breathing and heart rate?

10.— What is the chemical symbol for the element with atomic number 26?

11.— What is the phenomenon where light is bent as it passes through a medium with a different refractive index?

12.— Which gas makes up the majority of Earth's atmosphere?

13.— What is the unit of measurement for electric current?

14.— What is the study of fossils called?

15.— In the periodic table, which element has the chemical symbol K?

DID YOU KNOW ...

Turritopsis dohrnii, commonly known as the "immortal jellyfish," has the remarkable ability to revert its cells back to their earliest form and start its life cycle anew. This process can theoretically go on indefinitely, giving the jellyfish a form of biological immortality.

ANSWERS
1. Approximately 299,792 kilometers/second 2. Ohm 3. Sublimation 4. Transpiration 5. NaCl
6. Gamma rays 7. Approximately 343 meters per second 8. Stamen 9. Medulla oblongata 10. Fe (Iron)
11. Refraction 12. Nitrogen 13. Ampere 14. Paleontology 15. Potassium

GRAB BAG 2

1. — In astronomy, what is the term for a cluster of stars, gas, and dust bound together by gravity?

2. — In physics, what is the unit of measurement for force?

3. — What is the chemical symbol for lead?

4. — In biology, what is the process by which living organisms exchange gases with their environment, taking in oxygen and releasing carbon dioxide?

5. — What is the SI unit for measuring frequency?

6. — What is the name of the force that resists the relative motion of two surfaces in contact?

7. — What is the name of the subatomic particle that carries a negative electric charge and orbits the atomic nucleus?

8. — What is the chemical symbol for the element silver?

9. — In physics, what law states that the pressure of a gas is inversely proportional to its volume at a constant temperature?

10. — What is the SI unit for measuring temperature?

11. — In geology, what type of rock is formed from the cooling and solidification of magma or lava?

12. — In chemistry, what is the term for a substance that speeds up a chemical reaction without being consumed in the process?

13. — In geology, what is the term for the process of wearing away rock or soil by the action of wind, water, or ice?

14. — In astronomy, what is the name for the point in an orbit where a planet is farthest from the Sun?

15. — In genetics, what is the term for an alternative form of a gene that arises by mutation and is found at the same place on a chromosome?

DID YOU KNOW ...

Pando, located in Utah, is considered the world's oldest and heaviest living organism. It's a clonal colony of quaking aspen trees connected by a single root system, estimated to be thousands of years old.

ANSWERS
1. Galaxy 2. Newton (N) 3. Pb 4. Respiration 5.Hertz (Hz) 6. Friction 7. Electron 8. Ag 9. Boyle's Law
10. Kelvin (K) 11. Igneous rock 12. Catalyst 13. Erosion 14. Aphelion 15. Allele

GRAB BAG 3

1. — What is the process by which plants bend toward light?

2. — What is the unit of measurement for the intensity of sound waves?

3. — What is the process by which water changes from a gas to a liquid?

4. — What is the atomic number of the chemical element Neon (Ne)?

5. — In physics, what law states that an object at rest will stay at rest, and an object in motion will stay in motion unless acted upon by a net external force?

6. — In genetics, what term is used to describe the observable physical or biochemical characteristics of an organism, determined by its genetic makeup?

7. — What part of the brain is responsible for memory?

8. — In physics, what is the term for the force of attraction between two objects with mass, proportional to their masses and inversely proportional to the square of the distance between them?

9. — What is the primary element of the Earth's inner core, which is solid due to high pressure despite the high temperatures?

10.— In physics, what is the term for the property of matter that resists changes in its state of motion or rest?

11.— What is the name of the layer of the Earth's atmosphere, where the Northern and Southern Lights (auroras) occur?

12.— Who is known for the development of the periodic table of elements, organizing elements based on their atomic number?

13.— What medical researcher and virologist developed the first successful polio vaccine in the 1950s, contributing to the near-eradication of the disease?

14.— What is the largest organ internal organ in the human body?

15.— What is the chemical formula for hydrogen peroxide?

DID YOU KNOW ...

The average cumulus cloud can weigh up to a million pounds, which is about the same as the world's largest passenger jet.

ANSWERS
1. Phototropism 2. Decibel (dB) 3. Condensation 4. 10 5. Newton's first law of motion 6. Phenotype
7. Hippocampus 8. Gravity 9. Iron 10. Inertia 11. Thermosphere 12. Dmitri Mendeleev 13. Jonas Salk
14. Liver 15. H_2O_2

GRAB BAG 4

1. __ What term is used to describe the study of human cultures and societies?

2. __ What scientific instrument is used to measure atmospheric pressure?

3. __ What is the term for the layer of Earth's atmosphere where weather events, such as clouds and precipitation, occur?

4. __ In the taxonomic hierarchy, what comes next after species and groups together closely related species?

5. __ What is the name of the first operational space shuttle, launched by NASA in 1981?

6. __ Which psychologist is known for proposing the hierarchy of needs, which includes physiological, safety, love and belonging, esteem, and self-actualization needs?

7. __ In nuclear physics, what is the process by which a heavy atomic nucleus splits into two or more lighter nuclei?

8. __ Which scale is commonly used to measure the magnitude of earthquakes?

9. __ What is the process by which an organism develops from an egg to its adult form?

10.— In the human eye, what is the transparent, curved structure that helps focus light onto the retina?

11.— Who developed the theory of classical conditioning by conducting experiments with dogs, demonstrating the process of associative learning?

12.— What is the term for the speed and direction of an object's motion?

13.— Which mineral is the hardest naturally occurring substance on Earth?

14.— What is the name of the scale used to measure the intensity of tornadoes?

15.— In the scientific method, what is the term for the specific, testable statement that predicts the outcome of an experiment?

DID YOU KNOW ...

KIC 8462852, known as Tabby's Star, gained attention for its unusual light fluctuations observed by the Kepler Space Telescope. The cause of these irregular dips in brightness remains a mystery, leading to speculation about potential alien megastructures.

ANSWERS
1. Anthropology 2. Barometer 3. Troposphere 4. Genus 5.Space Shuttle Columbia 6. Abraham Maslow
7. Nuclear fission 8. Richter scale 9. Metamorphosis 10. Lens 11. Ivan Pavlov 12. Velocity 13. Diamond
14. The Enhanced Fujita Scale (EF Scale) 15. Hypothesis

7

FOOD & DRINK

NAME THE BRAND

1. — "Good to the last drop"

2. — "Melts in your mouth, not in your hands"

3. — "Betcha can't eat just one"

4. — "You're not you when you're hungry"

5. — "Think outside the bun"

6. — "They're grrreat!"

7. — "Spread the happy"

8. — "Eatin' good in the neighborhood"

9. — "Come hungry, leave happy"

10. — "Milk's favorite cookie"

11. — "Unexplainably juicy"

12. — "Theres no wrong way to eat a _______"

13. — "The taste you can see"

14. — "Sometimes you feel like a nut; sometimes you don't"

15. — "Is it in you?"

DID YOU KNOW ...

The "57" on Heinz ketchup bottles represents the number of varieties of pickles the company once advertised. H.J. Heinz chose the number 57 even though the company produced more than 57 products at the time. The phrase "57 varieties" became a successful marketing slogan for the brand.

ANSWERS
1. Maxwell House 2. M&M's 3. Lay's 4. Snickers 5.Taco Bell 6. Frosted Flakes 7. Nutella 8. Applebees
9. IHOP 10. Oreos 11. Starburst 12. Reese's 13. Cinnamon Toast Crunch 14. Almond Joy and Mounds
15. Gatorade

NAME THE FOOD

1. — What condiment was used in the 1830s as a medicine to treat ailments like diarrhea, indigestion, and jaundice?

2. — Which spice is made from the dried stigma of a flower and is one of the most expensive spices by weight?

3. — Which spice was one of the most sought-after and expensive during the Middle Ages, often referred to as "black gold"?

4. — Which fruit is known as the "king of fruits" and is notorious for its strong smell. A smell so strong it is banned in some hotels and public transportation?

5. — Originating in China, this fruit is often called a "Chinese gooseberry" and is known for its hairy brown skin?

6. — Which nut is used to make marzipan?

7. — The name for this popular dessert stems from the French word for "froth" or "foam"

8. — What ancient grain, known as the "golden grain of the Incas," is native to the Andes and is often ground into flour for various culinary uses?

9. — What italian dessert name translates to 'pick me up'?

10. — What fermented beverage, originating from China, is made from tea leaves, sugar, and a symbiotic culture of bacteria and yeast (SCOBY)?

11. — Lox is a fillet of the brined version of what type of what fish?

12. — What South American fruit, often called "the Amazonian grape," is a small, purple berry that grows on a palm tree and is rich in antioxidants?

13. — What type of food holds the world record for being the most stolen around the globe?

14. — What type of dried grape, smaller and darker than a raisin, is often used in baking and cooking, and is sometimes called a "Black Corinth"?

15. — What type of Italian pasta, resembling small rice grains, is often used in soups and is named after the Italian word for "barley"?

DID YOU KNOW ...

Fugu, or pufferfish, is a Japanese delicacy that is highly toxic if not prepared properly. Chefs must undergo extensive training and obtain a special license to serve fugu due to the potential danger. The liver and other organs of the fish contain a potent neurotoxin that can be fatal.

ANSWERS
1. Ketchup 2. Saffron 3. Pepper 4. Durian 5. Kiwi 6. Almonds 7. Mousse 8. Quinoa 9. Tiramisu
10. Kombucha 11. Salmon 12. Açaí Berry 13. Cheese 14. Currant. 15. Orzo

MOVIE & TV FOOD

1. — In "The Big Lebowski," what beverage does The Dude drink?

2. — In "The Godfather," what dish is being prepared and maned here: "Leave the gun, take the ________".

3. — In "Elf," what food group does Buddy remind everyone is the main food group of elves?

4. — In "Pulp Fiction," what fast-food restaurant do Vincent and Mia go to for a $5 shake?

5. — In "The Simpsons Movie," what fast-food item does Homer try to eat multiple times at the Krusty Burger?

6. — In "Harry Potter and the Philosopher's Stone," what magical candy does Harry buy on the Hogwarts Express from the trolley witch?

7. — In "Seinfeld," what food does George buy Elaine, but becomes upset at his girlfriend for supposedly taking the credit for buying?

8. — In "The Princess and the Frog," what dish does Tiana prepare that turns her into a frog?

9. — In "The Breakfast Club," what does John Bender use to create a makeshift sandwich during detention?

10. — In "Bridesmaids," what unusual flavor does Annie give to the cupcakes she bakes for her best friend's bridal shower?

11. — In "Friends," what is the name of Ross's Thanksgiving sandwich, consisting of a leftover Thanksgiving meal?

12. — In "Julie & Julia," what classic French dish does Julie struggle to master in her quest to cook through Julia Child's cookbook?

13. — In "The Goonies," what candy bar does Chuck toss Sloth that leads to Sloth breaking out of his chains?

14. — In "The Martian," what food does Mark Watney grow on Mars to sustain himself?

15. — In "Raiders of the Lost Ark," what type of food does Monkey Man try to poison Indiana Jones with?

DID YOU KNOW ...

The character of the Soup Nazi on "Seinfeld" was inspired by a real soup vendor in New York City known for his strict rules. The real-life soup vendor, Al Yeganeh, did not appreciate the portrayal and initially banned the show's creators from his soup stand.

ANSWERS
1. White Russian 2. Cannoli 3. Candy 4. Jack Rabbit Slim's 5. The Krusty Burger's "Clogger"
6. Chocolate Frogs 7. The Big Salad 8. Beignets 9. Pixy Stix and Captain Crunch cereal
10. Carrot with lemon 11. The Moist Maker 12. Beef Bourguignon 13. Baby Ruth 14. Potatoes 15. Dates

GRAB BAG

1. — In the 1960s, what candy made its debut with the slogan "Makes Mouths Happy"?

2. — What popular breakfast cereal was created by Dr. John Harvey Kellogg as a health food at the Battle Creek Sanitarium in the late 19th century?

3. — Which country claims to be the birthplace of coffee, with legends attributing its discovery to a 9th-century goat herder named Kaldi?

4. — Which beverage was initially created as a medicinal tonic in 1886 by Dr. John Stith Pemberton?

5. — For Tariff purposes, In 1893 The U.S. Supreme Court ruled that this fruit should be classified as a vegetable

6. — What pepper is named as the spiciest pepper on earth, according to the Guiness book of world records?

7. — What year did the first McDonald's restaurant open its doors?

8. — Which soft drink brand used the slogan "The Uncola" in the 1970s?

9. — Which iconic TV dinner was introduced in 1954 and included turkey, stuffing, and sweet potatoes?

10.— What ancient civilization is credited with inventing beer over 5,000 years ago?

11.— Who is the chef and host of the television show "No Reservations" and "Parts Unknown"?

12.— Who is the famous chef known as the "Naked Chef"?

13.— Which country is credited with the invention of ice cream in the 8th century?

14.— What year did the first mass-produced chocolate bar become available to the public?

15.— What is the national dish of Spain?

DID YOU KNOW ...

Tea bags were invented by accident in the early 20th century. In 1908, Thomas Sullivan, a New York tea merchant, sent samples of tea to his customers in small silk bags. Some customers mistakenly placed the entire bag into hot water, leading to the unintentional creation of the tea bag.

ANSWERS
1. Twizzlers 2. Corn Flakes 3. Ethiopia 4. Coca-Cola 5. Tomato 6. Pepper X (as of October of 2023)
7. 1940 8. 7UP 9. Swanson TV Dinner 10. Sumerians 11. Anthony Bourdain 12. Jamie Oliver 13. China
14. 1866 15. Paella

ALCOHOL YOU LATER

1. — What is the term for the study of wines, including their production, storage, and tasting?

2. — In what year was the word "cocktail" first used in print?

3. — What is the name of the tequila brand co-founded by actor George Clooney?

4. — What is the name of the beer brand with the slogan "The World's Most Refreshing Beer"?

5. — What is the proper term for the foam that forms on the top of a beer when poured into a glass?

6. — In what year did Prohibition officially begin in the United States with the ratification of the 18th Amendment?

7. — What is the main ingredient in gin that gives it its distinctive flavor?

8. — Which anise-flavored spirit is known as "The Green Fairy" and was famously associated with artists and writers in the 19th and 20th centuries?

9. — Which rum brand uses the slogan "Live Passionately. Drink Responsibly."?

10.— Which wine-producing region in France is known for its iconic red wines made from Cabernet Sauvignon, Merlot, and Cabernet Franc grapes?

11.— What is the name of the ancient Sumerian goddess associated with beer, considered the mother of all beer?

12.— In what year did National Minimum Drinking Age Act standardize the drinking age to 21 across all states?

13.— What wine term is used to describe the scent or aroma of a wine, often associated with the grape variety and the winemaking process?

14.— Which beer company's advertising campaign featured the tagline "Good Things Come to Those Who Wait"?

15.— Which beer company's advertising campaign featured the tagline "Open Your World"?

DID YOU KNOW ...

Bees are attracted to alcohol. Researchers have found that bees are drawn to the scent of fermented nectar, and they may occasionally indulge in small amounts of alcohol. Some plants produce fermented nectar naturally, and bees might consume it while foraging.

ANSWERS
1. Oenology 2. 1798 3. Casamigos 4. Coors Light 5. Head 6. 1920 7. Juniper berries 8. Absinthe
9. Bacardi 10. Bordeaux 11. Ninkasi 12. 1984 13. Bouquet 14. Guinness 15. Heineken

GRAB BAG 2

1. — Which celebrity chef is famous for his "BAM!" catchphrase and his Cajun and Creole cuisine?

2. — Which gas is commonly used in food packaging to slow down the oxidation process and extend shelf life?

3. — Which country is famous for producing Roquefort cheese, a type of blue cheese made from sheep's milk?

4. — Which type of food preservation involves removing moisture to inhibit the growth of microorganisms?

5. — What is the unit of measurement for spiciness in food?

6. — Which gas is responsible for causing bread to rise during the process of leavening?

7. — What is the name of the traditional Scottish dish made with minced meat and oatmeal?

8. — What prestigious award is often referred to as the "Oscars of the food world"?

9. — Which beverage brand urges you to "Obey your thirst"?

10.— Who is the chef and host of the television series "Hell's Kitchen," known for his tough demeanor and high culinary standards?

11.— What cereal brand promises that "They're magically delicious"?

12.— Which city in France is known as the gastronomic capital of the world and is famous for its Michelin-starred restaurants

13.— What macronutrient is primarily responsible for providing energy in the form of calories?

14.— What fictional restaurant is known for its "Krabby Patty" burger?

15.— What is the name of the restaurant located at the top of the Eiffel Tower in Paris?

DID YOU KNOW ...

The cashew nut grows on the end of a cashew apple. Interestingly, the shell of the cashew nut contains a substance called urushiol, which is the same irritant found in poison ivy. Roasting the cashews helps neutralize this substance.

ANSWERS
1. Emeril Lagasse 2. Nitrogen 3. France 4. Dehydration 5. Scoville Heat Units (SHU) 6. Carbon dioxide
7. Haggis 8. The James Beard Awards 9. Sprite 10. Gordon Ramsay 11. Lucky Charms (General Mills)
12. Lyon 13. Carbohydrate 14. The Krusty Krab (SpongeBob SquarePants) 15. The Jules Verne

GRAB BAG 3

1. __ Which country is the largest consumer of chocolate per capita?

2. __ What is the term for the outer layer of grain that is removed during the milling process?

3. __ Which Italian dessert, often served alongside or atop ice cream, consists of espresso poured over a scoop of vanilla ice cream?

4. __ Which fast-food chain is famous for its "Double-Double" and "Animal Style" options?

5. __ Who is credited with inventing the process of pasteurization to prevent spoilage in wine and beer?

6. __ What iconic American snack food was invented by George Crum in the 19th century as a response to a customer's complaint about thick French fries?

7. __ Which fruit contains an enzyme called bromelain that can break down proteins and tenderize meat?

8. __ What year was the Oreo introduced?

9. __ What popular chocolate and nougat candy bar is often associated with a distinctive, triangular shape?

10. — What classic French sauce is made from egg yolks, butter, and lemon juice, and is often served with seafood?

11. — Who is often regarded as the "Father of Modern French Cuisine" and wrote the culinary classic "Le Guide Culinaire"?

12. — What is the maximum number of Michelin stars a restaurant can receive?

13. — What Japanese chef is credited with popularizing sushi worldwide and owns the acclaimed sushi restaurant Sukiyabashi Jiro in Tokyo?

14. — Which Roman emperor is said to have been poisoned with a dish known as "Amanita caesarea," a type of edible mushroom?

15. — What is the name of the yogurt-based sauce commonly used in Middle Eastern cuisine, often served with grilled meats or as a dip?

DID YOU KNOW ...

The name "Kit Kat" is believed to have originated from the 18th-century Kit-Cat Club, a London literary and political club. The creators of the chocolate bar wanted a distinctive name that would be easily recognizable and memorable.

ANSWERS
1. Switzerland 2. Bran 3. Affogato 4. In-N-Out Burger 5. Louis Pasteur 6. Potato chips 7. Pineapple
8. 1912 9. Toblerone 10. Hollandaise sauce 11. Georges Auguste Escoffier 12. 3 13. Jiro Ono
14. Claudius 15. Tzatziki

8

MYTHOLOGY & FOLKLORE

GREEK MYTHOLOGY

1. — Who is the god of the sea and earthquakes in Greek mythology?

2. — Which winged horse is often associated with the Muses and sprang from the blood of Medusa when she was slain by Perseus?

3. — Who is the goddess of love and beauty, born from the sea foam after Uranus's castration?

4. — What three sisters share one eye among them and are the daughters of the sea god Phorcys and the goddess Ceto?

5. — What is the name of the ferryman who transports souls across the river Styx to the Underworld?

6. — Who is the goddess of the harvest, agriculture, and fertility?

7. — What creature is part lion, part goat, and part serpent, famously slain by Bellerophon with the help of Pegasus?

8. — Which goddess of the rainbow is the messenger of the gods and connects the mortal world with Mount Olympus?

9. — Who is the god of war, son of Zeus and Hera, known for his destructive and unpredictable nature?

10.— Who is the god of wine, parties, and festivities in Greek mythology?

11.— What is the name of the fire-breathing, hundred-headed serpent defeated by Heracles as one of his labors?

12.— Which Titan was punished by Zeus to hold up the sky for eternity?

13.— Who is the queen of the underworld and the wife of Hades?

14.— Which hero, known for his intelligence, devised the Trojan Horse and was central to the fall of Troy?

15.— Which hero is known for slaying the Gorgon Medusa?

DID YOU KNOW ...

Harpies were mythical creatures with the bodies of birds and the heads of women. They were often depicted as wind spirits, and their name means "snatchers" in Greek, reflecting their role in swiftly carrying away the souls of the dead.

ANSWERS
1. Poseidon 2. Pegasus 3. Aphrodite 4. The Graeae 5. Charon 6. Demeter 7. Chimera 8. Iris 9. Ares
10. Dionysus 11. Hydra 12. Atlas 13. Persephone 14. Odysseus 15. Perseus

NORSE MYTHOLOGY

1. — What powerful race of female beings determines the fates of gods and mortals in Norse mythology?

2. — Who is the god of war, glory, and death in Norse mythology, and is associated with Valhalla?

3. — Which thunder god wields the mighty hammer Mjolnir and is the son of Odin?

4. — Which god is associated with the sea and seafaring and is ruler of the ocean?

5. — Who is the goddess of love and beauty in Norse mythology?

6. — What is the name of the sacred tree that connects the nine worlds?

7. — What is the name of the eight-legged horse that Odin rides?

8. — What is the name of the giant serpent that encircles the world in Norse mythology?

9. — What is the name of the eternal winter that precedes Ragnarok?

10.— Who is the trickster god, shape-shifter, and mischief-maker in Norse mythology?

11.— What is the name of the legendary wolf bound by the gods, foretold to break free during Ragnarok?

12.— Who are the divine blacksmiths and craftsmen in Norse mythology, known for creating powerful artifacts?

13.— Which realm is the home of the Aesir gods?

14.— Who are the three brothers who created the world in Norse mythology?

15.— Who is the giantess and mother of Loki's children, Hel, Jörmungandr, and Fenrir?

DID YOU KNOW ...

Yggdrasil, the World Tree in Norse mythology, has three roots that extend into different realms. One root reaches Asgard (home of the gods), another reaches Jotunheim (realm of the giants), and the third reaches Helheim (realm of the dead). Near these roots are sacred wells: Urdarbrunnr (well of fate), Mímisbrunnr (well of wisdom), and Hvergelmir (roaring kettle).

ANSWERS
1. Norns 2. Odin 3. Thor 4. Njord 5. Freyja 6. Yggdrasil 7. Sleipnir 8. Jormungandr
9. Fimbulwinter(Fimbulvetr) 10. Loki 11. Fenrir 12. Dwarves 13. Asgard 14. Odin, Vili, and Ve
15. Angrboda

ROMAN MYTHOLOGY

1. — What is the Roman name for the goddess of the Earth and fertility?

2. — Who is the king of the Roman gods in Roman mythology?

3. — What is the Roman name for the god of love and desire?

4. — In Roman mythology, who is the guardian spirit of a place, often depicted as a snake?

5. — Who is the Roman virgin goddess of wisdom, medicine, the arts, poetry, and handicrafts?

6. — Who is the Roman god of wine and revelry?

7. — What is the Roman name for the god of the sun?

8. — Who is the messenger of the gods in Roman mythology?

9. — In Roman mythology, what is the name of the goddess of the moon?

10.— In Roman mythology, what is the name of the fire god?

11.— In Roman mythology, what is the name of the god of time and the ages?

12.— In Roman mythology, what is the name of the god of the sea?

13.— What is the name of the Roman goddess of the dawn?

14.— In Roman mythology, what is the name of the god of the underworld?

15.— What is the Roman name for the three sisters who controlled human destiny?

DID YOU KNOW ...

Janus was a unique Roman god who had two faces, one looking forward and the other looking backward. He was the god of beginnings, transitions, and doorways. Janus was often invoked during important events like marriages and the opening of new ventures.

ANSWERS
1. Terra Mater 2. Jupiter 3. Cupid 4. Genius Loci 5. Minerva 6. Bacchus 7. Sol 8. Mercury 9. Luna
10. Vulcan 11. Saturn 12. Neptune 13. Aurora 14. Pluto 15. The Parcae

MYTHICAL CREATURES

1. — What mythical creature in Arab folklore is a desert-dwelling bird with a wingspan large enough to block the sun?

2. — In Native American folklore, what creature is a shape-shifter and often considered a trickster figure?

3. — In Hindu mythology, what creature is a giant eagle and the mount of the god Vishnu?

4. — What creature in Greek mythology is a giant with a hundred eyes, who serves as a watchman for the gods?

5. — What mythical creature is known for luring sailors with enchanting songs and causing shipwrecks?

6. — What legendary creature is said to have the body of a lion and the wings of an eagle?

7. — What legendary creature in Scottish folklore is said to inhabit lochs, with Nessie being a famous example?

8. — What creature in Hindu mythology is part elephant and part human?

9. — In Greek mythology, what creature is part lion, part goat, and part serpent?

10.— Which legendary bird is said to rise from its ashes after dying in Greek mythology?

11.— In Japanese mythology, what turtle has a long tail of seaweed, is said to be 10,000 years old and represents longevity and wisdom?

12.— What mythical creature in Irish folklore is a shape-shifting, water spirit that inhabits lakes and rivers, often described as grey or white horse-like creatures that can take human form?

13.— In Egyptian mythology, what mythical creature has the body of a lion and the head of a pharaoh?

14.— In Chinese mythology, who is the dragon god of the tempest and master of rain?

15.— In Greek mythology, what creature is a half-man, half-horse known for its wisdom and healing abilities?

DID YOU KNOW ...

Amabie is a yokai (spirit) from Japanese folklore with a beak, long hair, and fish scales. According to legend, Amabie appeared from the sea and prophesied an epidemic. During the COVID-19 pandemic, images of Amabie resurfaced in Japan as a symbol of protection and hope.

ANSWERS
1. Roc 2. Coyote 3. Garuda 4. Argos (or Argus Panoptes) 5. Siren 6. Griffin 7. Loch Ness Monster
8. Ganesha 9. Chimera 10. Phoenix 11. Minogame 12. Kelpie 13. Sphinx 14. Shenlong 15. Centaur

FOLKLORE

1. — What Central American folklore creature has a name that translates to 'goat-sucker'?

2. — What folklore figure, often portrayed as a supernatural being with a lantern, guides travelers at night and is associated with marshes?

3. — What folklore figure, often depicted as a hag or witch, is known for flying on a mortar and pestle and causing mischief?

4. — In Native American folklore, what creature is a mythical, giant bird that creates thunder with its wings and is associated with storms?

5. — What folklore figure, often depicted as a mischievous trickster, is known for its association with crossroads and often portrayed with a fiddle in American folklore?

6. — In Slavic folklore, what supernatural being is a house spirit that protects the household and its occupants?

7. — What folklore creature, popular in English mythology, is a small, winged humanoid often associated with granting wishes?

8. — In Irish folklore, what mischievous fairy creature is known for cobbling shoes while people sleep?

9. — In Japanese folklore, what supernatural creature is a shape-shifting fox with magical abilities?

10. — What folklore figure, often depicted as a fairy or spirit, is known for granting three wishes to those who set it free from captivity?

11. — What folklore figure, often depicted as a horned, goat-like creature, is associated with the medieval concept of the devil?

12. — What legendary creature, originating from Celtic mythology, is believed to inhabit rural areas and is known for dancing and leading travelers astray?

13. — What folklore figure, often depicted as a hairy, ape-like creature, is said to inhabit remote forests and mountains?

14. — What folklore figure, often depicted as a malevolent spirit with the ability to shape-shift, is known for its eerie, night-time wailing?

15. — In Greek mythology, what creature is a half-man, half-bull monster confined within the labyrinth on the island of Crete?

DID YOU KNOW ...

The legend of the Green Children of Woolpit tells the story of two siblings with green skin who reportedly appeared in the English village of Woolpit during the 12th century. According to folklore, they spoke an unknown language and claimed to come from an underground world with a green-lit sky.

GRAB BAG

1. — What herb is believed to keep ghosts away if rubbed on the body and kept close while sleeping?

2. — Which gemstone is often believed to have protective qualities against negative energies and is associated with balancing emotions?

3. — What metal is thought to have protective properties against supernatural entities, and is often used in folklore to create talismans?

4. — What ancient symbol, often associated with protection and warding off evil, consists of an eye enclosed in a triangle?

5. — In folklore, what type of footwear is believed to bring good luck and is often placed upside down to prevent the luck from escaping?

6. — In folklore, what is often worn as a pendant and is believed to protect against the evil eye and negative energies?

7. — In traditional Chinese folklore, what animal is associated with good luck, prosperity, and is a symbol of the Chinese New Year?

8. — What practice involves using the smoke from burning herbs, plants, or resins for spiritual or cleansing purposes?

9. — What serpentine creature is said to be vulnerable to meeting its own gaze? Hunters of this creature would often carry mirrors

10.— Who is known as a skilled lumberjack with a companion, Babe the Blue Ox?

11.— What plant is associated with werewolf lore, believed to have properties that can harm or repel werewolves?

12.— It is believed that by drinking water from this source will a person will be eternally young

13.— In Hindu mythology, who is the god of destruction?

14.— In Greek mythology, who is the goddess of wisdom and warfare?

15.— What is the name of the three-headed dog guarding the Underworld in Greek mythology?

DID YOU KNOW ...

In magical traditions, creating dream pillows filled with specific herbs is believed to enhance dreams or bring about certain qualities. For example, placing herbs like lavender for relaxation or mugwort for lucid dreaming inside a pillow was thought to influence the dreamer's experience during sleep.

ANSWERS
1. Mugwort 2. Amethyst 3. Iron 4. Eye of Providence or Eye or Horus 5. Horseshoe 6. Amulet 7. Dragon
8. Smudging 9. Basilisk 10. Paul Bunyan 11. Wolfsbane 12. Fountain of Youth 13. Shiva. 14. Athena
15. Cerberus

GRAB BAG 2

1. — In Roman mythology, who is the god of war?

2. — What mythical creature in Middle Eastern folklore is a female demon associated with seduction and temptation?

3. — What legendary creature in Australian Aboriginal mythology is a giant, mythical being often associated with the creation of landscapes?

4. — In Egyptian mythology, who is the god of the afterlife and the judge of the dead?

5. — In Hindu mythology, who is the monkey god known for his strength and loyalty to Lord Rama?

6. — What legendary sea monster in Roman mythology is said to dwell in the Straits of Messina, threatening sailors and ships?

7. — What mythical creature from Persian folklore is a hybrid of a lion and eagle with the wings of a bird of prey?

8. — What is the name of the monstrous sea serpent in Scandinavian folklore that terrorizes sailors?

9. — Who is the god of the sun and one of the most important deities in Egyptian mythology?

10.— In Hawaiian mythology, what goddess is associated with fire, volcanoes, and the creation of the Hawaiian Islands?

11.— In Norse mythology, what is the name of Thor's enchanted hammer?

12.— What legendary figure is believed to be a supernatural entity that appears in mirrors when summoned, often associated with horror folklore?

13.— In Egyptian mythology, who is the god of the sky, often depicted with a falcon head?

14.— In Brazilian folklore, what creature is a shape-shifting dolphin that transforms into a handsome man to woo and marry human women?

15.— What mythical creature from Japanese folklore is a shape-shifting raccoon dog with magical abilities?

DID YOU KNOW ...

In Icelandic folklore, the Huldufólk, or "hidden people," are believed to be supernatural beings that inhabit the rocks, hills, and fields of Iceland. Descriptions of the Huldufólk vary, but they're often depicted as beautiful and sometimes invisible to humans. Many Icelanders still hold beliefs about these hidden folk, and road construction projects have even been altered to avoid disturbing their supposed habitats.

ANSWERS
1. Mars 2. Succubus 3. Rainbow Serpent 4. Osiris 5. Hanuman 6. Scylla 7. Griffin 8. Kraken 9. Ra 10. Pele 11. Mjolnir 12. Bloody Mary 13. Horus 14. Boto 15. Tanuki

9

HISTORY

WORLD WAR I

1. — In what year did World War I begin?

2. — What was the name of the ship sunk by a German submarine, leading to the United States entering World War I?

3. — Which country withdrew from World War I in 1917 due to internal revolutions?

4. — What was the nickname given to American soldiers who fought in World War I?

5. — What was the name of the treaty that ended the state of war between Germany and the Allied Powers in 1920?

6. — Which country, after initially declaring neutrality, joined the Allies in 1915?

7. — What was the name of the secret agreement between Britain, France, and Russia, outlining their intentions for the post-war division of the Ottoman Empire?

8. — Which famous assassination in 1914 is often considered a precursor to World War I?

9. — Which country experienced the "Easter Rising" in 1916, seeking independence from British rule during World War I?

10.— Who was the leader of the Bolshevik Revolution in Russia during World War I?

11.— What was the term used to describe the system of fortified trenches that stretched from the Belgian coast to the Swiss border during World War I?

12.— Which world leader proposed the idea of the League of Nations?

13.— Who was the British Prime Minister during most of World War I?

14.— What was the nickname of the British Mark I tank, the world's first tank used in battle?

15.— Which battle, fought from February to December 1916, saw the longest single battle in World War I?

DID YOU KNOW ...

During the war, trenches were infested with rats, leading to the deployment of "trench cats" by some soldiers. Cats were kept to control the rat population and provided companionship to the troops.

ANSWERS
1. 1914 2. Lusitania 3. Russia 4. Doughboys 5. Treaty of Versailles 6. Italy 7. The Sykes-Picot Agreement
8. The assassination of Archduke Franz Ferdinand of Austria-Hungary 9. Ireland 10. Vladimir Lenin
11. The Western Front 12. Woodrow Wilson 13. David Lloyd George 14. 'Mother'
15. The Battle of Verdun

WORLD WAR II

1. — Which two countries signed the Molotov-Ribbentrop Pact, a non-aggression treaty, just before the outbreak of World War II?

2. — What was the code name for the Allied invasion of Normandy on June 6, 1944?

3. — In which year did the United States enter World War II?

4. — What was the code name for the project that developed the atomic bomb during World War II?

5. — Which European city was known as the "Bridge Too Far" during an unsuccessful Allied military operation?

6. — What year did World War II begin?

7. — What was the name of the famous U.S. aircraft that dropped the atomic bomb on Hiroshima on August 6, 1945?

8. — What was the codename for the German invasion of the Soviet Union in June 1941?

9. — Which country was invaded by Germany on April 9, 1940, leading to its surrender within two months?

10.— Which battle in the Pacific, fought in June 1942, halted Japanese expansion and marked the end of their advance?

11.— What was the name of the U.S. program that provided financial and material support to help rebuild Western European economies after World War II?

12.— Which battle, fought in the winter of 1944-1945, was the last major German offensive on the Western Front?

13.— Which Allied power was led by General Charles de Gaulle during World War II?

14.— Which Soviet city was besieged by German forces for over 870 days during World War II?

15.— Which operation involved the mass evacuation of Allied soldiers from the beaches of Dunkirk in 1940?

DID YOU KNOW ...

During the war, the Allies created a "Ghost Army," officially known as the 23rd Headquarters Special Troops. Comprising artists, designers, and sound engineers, this unit used inflatable tanks, sound effects, and other deceptive tactics to mislead the German forces about the location and strength of Allied units. Their efforts played a role in the success of various military operations.

ANSWERS
1. Germany and the Soviet Union 2. Operation Overlord 3. 1941 4. The Manhattan Project
5. Arnhem (Operation Market Garden) 6. 1939 7. Enola Gay 8. Operation Barbarossa 9. Denmark
10. The Battle of Midway 11.The Marshall Plan 12. The Battle of the Bulge 13. Free French Forces
14. Leningrad (modern-day St. Petersburg) 15. Operation Dynamo

RECENT HISTORY

1. — What was the name of the mission that successfully landed NASA's Perseverance rover on Mars in 2021?

2. — Which country hosted the 2021 Summer Olympics?

3. — What major agreement aimed at addressing climate change was reached in 2015?

4. — In 2016, the United Kingdom held a referendum to decide whether to leave or remain in the European Union. What was this referendum commonly known as?

5. — In 2017, Hurricane Harvey caused widespread flooding in which major U.S. city?

6. — In 2021, a container ship called Ever Given blocked the Suez Canal. In which country did this incident occur?

7. — In 2012, what was the name of the rover that successfully landed on Mars to explore its surface?

8. — The JCPOA, an international agreement regarding Iran's nuclear program, was signed in 2015. What does JCPOA stand for?

9. — In 2011, a royal wedding captured the world's attention. Which prince married Catherine Middleton?

10.— In 2019, the Nobel Peace Prize was awarded to the Prime Minister of Ethiopia for his efforts to achieve peace with which neighboring country?

11.— In 2012, scientists at CERN announced the discovery of a particle consistent with the Higgs boson. What is the popular nickname for this particle?

12.— What cryptocurrency, introduced in 2009, is often considered the first decentralized digital currency?

13.— In 2020, SpaceX successfully launched astronauts into space, marking the first crewed orbital launch by a private company. What was the name of the spacecraft used?

14.— The G7 is a group of seven major advanced economies. Which country hosted the G7 Summit in 2018?

15.— Malala Yousafzai, an advocate for girls' education, won the Nobel Peace Prize in 2014. Which country is she from?

DID YOU KNOW ...

In 1990, two thieves dressed as police officers entered the Isabella Stewart Gardner Museum in Boston and stole 13 pieces of artwork, including works by Vermeer and Rembrandt. The artworks remain missing, and the case is one of the most significant unsolved art thefts in history.

ANSWERS
1. The Mars 2020 Mission 2. Japan (Tokyo) 3. The Paris Agreement 4. Brexit referendum
5. Houston, Texas 6. Egypt 7. Curiosity (Mars Science Laboratory) 8. Joint Comprehensive Plan of Action
9. Prince William 10. Eritrea 11. 'god particle' 12. Bitcoin 13. The Crew Dragon Endeavor 14. Canada
15. Pakistan

ANCIENT CIVILIZATIONS

1. — What ancient civilization is known for constructing massive stone heads on Easter Island?

2. — Which ancient Egyptian pharaoh is famous for building the Great Pyramid of Giza?

3. — What ancient civilization developed the world's first known writing system, known as cuneiform?

4. — Which ancient Greek city-state is known for its military prowess and the Battle of Thermopylae?

5. — What ancient city was the capital of the Inca Empire and is now a UNESCO World Heritage Site?

6. — What ancient Indian scripture, composed in Sanskrit, is a collection of hymns and religious rituals?

7. — In ancient Egypt, who was the queen known for her alliance with Mark Antony and her tragic end with a snakebite?

8. — What ancient Mesoamerican civilization built the city of Chichen Itza and developed the calendar system?

9. — What ancient Persian king is known for his military campaigns and the construction of Persepolis?

10.— In ancient Greece, who is considered the "Father of Medicine" and established the Hippocratic Oath?

11.— What ancient Mesopotamian city is famous for its ziggurat, the Tower of Babel, and the Epic of Gilgamesh?

12.— Which ancient civilization is credited with the creation of the Rosetta Stone, allowing for the decipherment of hieroglyphs?

13.— What ancient Greek city-state is the birthplace of democracy and the philosopher Socrates?

14.— In ancient Rome, who was the legendary founder and first king of Rome?

15.— In ancient Mesopotamia, what is the name of the sacred temple tower that served as a religious center?

DID YOU KNOW ...

The Indus Valley Civilization, one of the world's oldest urban cultures, left behind a written script on seals and artifacts. However, as of now, researchers have been unable to decipher the script. The mystery of the Indus Valley script adds intrigue to our understanding of this ancient civilization.

ANSWERS
1. Rapa Nui 2. Pharaoh Khufu 3. Sumerians 4. Sparta 5. Cuzco, Peru 6. The Rigveda 7. Cleopatra 8. Maya civilization (Mayans) 9. Darius 10. Hippocrates 11.Babylon 12. Ancient Egyptians 13. Athens 14. Romulus 15. Ziggurat

WORLD RULERS

1. — Who was the last Tsar of Russia, whose reign ended with the Russian Revolution of 1917?

2. — Which leader, known as the "Father of the Nation," led India to independence through nonviolent civil disobedience?

3. — What Roman Emperor, known for building the Colosseum, ruled from 69 to 79 AD and was the last of the Flavian dynasty?

4. — Which leader, known as "The Iron Lady," served as the Prime Minister of the United Kingdom from 1979 to 1990?

5. — Which ancient Indian emperor is known for spreading Buddhism across Asia and erecting stone pillars with edicts?

6. — Who was the longest reigning monarch in British history?

7. — Who was the first Emperor of China, known for unifying the country in 221 BC?

8. — What ancient Roman general crossed the Rubicon River, leading to the downfall of the Roman Republic and the rise of the Roman Empire?

9. — What state was Franklin Roosevelt born in?

10. — Who was the longest-reigning monarch in French history, ruling for over 72 years during the Bourbon Restoration?

11. — What Mongol leader founded the Yuan Dynasty in China and is known for his conquests across Asia and Europe?

12. — What medieval English king is known for his role in the Hundred Years' War and the Battle of Agincourt?

13. — Who was the longest-reigning monarch in Japanese history, serving as Emperor for over 63 years?

14. — Who was the ancient Greek general and conqueror who created one of the largest empires in history?

15. — What event in 1066 marked the Norman conquest of England and the crowning of William the Conqueror as king?

DID YOU KNOW ...

Queen Nzinga, a 17th-century ruler of the Ndongo and Matamba kingdoms in Central Africa (present-day Angola), was known for her diplomatic skills. She successfully negotiated with Portuguese colonizers, often employing strategic alliances and political maneuvering to resist European influence in the region.

ANSWERS
1. Nicholas II 2. Mahatma Gandhi 3. Vespasian 4. Margaret Thatcher 5. Ashoka the Great
6. Queen Elizabeth II 7. Qin Shi Huangdi 8. Julius Caesar 9. New York 10. King Louis XIV 11.Kublai Khan
12. King Henry V 13. Emperor Hirohito 14. Alexander the Great 15. Battle of Hastings

GRAB BAG

1. — Who was the founder of the Mongol Empire?

2. — What was the term used to describe the geopolitical division between the democratic and capitalist West, led by the United States, and the communist East, led by the Soviet Union during the Cold War?

3. — What ancient Greek historian is often referred to as the "Father of History" and wrote "Histories"?

4. — Which revolution in 1917 led to the overthrow of the Russian Provisional Government and the establishment of the first socialist state in the world?

5. — In what year did the Black Death, a devastating pandemic, reach Europe and result in the deaths of millions of people?

6. — What major event occurred on July 14, 1789, when revolutionaries stormed a prison in Paris, symbolizing the start of the French Revolution?

7. — Who was the ancient Greek philosopher known for his teachings on ethics and the concept of the "golden mean"?

8. — In what year did the Treaty of Versailles officially end World War I?

9. — What was the slogan associated with the American Revolution, reflecting the desire for self-governance and independence from British rule?

10.— What revolutionary leader played a central role in the Cuban Revolution and became the Prime Minister and later the President of Cuba?

11.— What famous explorer led the first circumnavigation of the Earth from 1519 to 1522?

12.— What was the name of the mission that led to astronauts Neil Armstrong and Buzz Aldrin becoming the first humans to walk on the Moon on July 20, 1969?

13.— What medieval conflict between England and France lasted from 1337 to 1453 and was characterized by battles such as Agincourt?

14.— What famous Scottish patriot led the Wars of Scottish Independence against English rule and is depicted in the movie "Braveheart"?

15.— What European monarch is known for the construction of the Palace of Versailles and his absolutist rule in France?

DID YOU KNOW ...

Cliometrics is an approach to historical research that applies quantitative methods to analyze historical data. This approach, rooted in economics, aims to test historical hypotheses through statistical analysis. It has been used to study various historical phenomena, including economic trends, demographic patterns, and social structures.

ANSWERS
1. Genghis Khan 2. The Iron Curtain. 3. Herodotus
4. The October Revolution (also known as the Bolshevik Revolution) 5. 1347 6. The Storming of the Bastille
7. Aristotle. 8. 1919 9. "No taxation without representation" 10. Fidel Castro 11. Ferdinand Magellan
12. Apollo 11 13. The Hundred Years' War 14. William Wallace 15. Louis XIV

NAME THE YEAR

1. — The establishment of the European Union

2. — The signing of the Magna Carta

3. — The first successful cloning of a mammal, Dolly the sheep

4. — The construction of the Eiffel Tower in Paris is completed

5. — The first image of a black hole is captured by the Event Horizon Telescope

6. — The first modern olympics is held

7. — The establishment of the World Health Organization (WHO)

8. — The first successful human mission to the International Space Station (ISS)

9. — The publication of Isaac Newton's "Philosophiæ Naturalis Principia Mathematica," laying the foundation for classical mechanics

10.— The fall of Constantinople to the Ottoman Empire

11.— The first successful human organ transplant, a kidney

12.— The publication of Charles Darwin's "On the Origin of Species"

13.— The assassination of President Abraham Lincoln at Ford's Theatre in Washington, D.C.

14.— The Great Fire of London

15.— The Kyoto Protocol, an international treaty aimed at addressing climate change, is adopted

DID YOU KNOW ...

In the summer of 1518 in Strasbourg, Alsace (modern-day France), a mysterious event known as the Dancing Plague occurred. People began to dance uncontrollably in the streets, and the phenomenon spread, affecting hundreds. The cause remains unclear, with theories ranging from mass hysteria to ergot poisoning.

ANSWERS
1. 1993 **2.** 1215 **3.** 1996 **4.** 1889 **5.** 2019 **6.** 1896 **7.** 1948 **8.** 2000 **9.** 1687 **10.** 1453 **11.**1954 **12.** 1859
13. 1865 **14.** 1666 **15.** 1997

10
POP CULTURE

STAGE NAMES

1. — Reginald Kenneth Dwight

2. — Stefani Joanne Angelina Germanotta

3. — Robyn Fenty

4. — Katheryn Elizabeth Hudson

5. — Peter Gene Hernandez

6. — Robert Allen Zimmerman

7. — Shawn Corey Carter

8. — Paul David Hewson

9. — Eric Marlon Bishop

10. — Dwayne Michael Carter Jr.

11. — Richard Starkey

12. — Eileen Regina Edwards

13. — Norma Jean Mortenson

14. — Calvin Cordozar Broadus Jr.

15. — Vincent Damon Furnier

DID YOU KNOW ...

The acclaimed actor Joaquin Phoenix was born Joaquin Rafael Bottom. After his family became part of the Children of God religious cult, they changed their last name to Phoenix, symbolizing a new beginning. Joaquin took the first name "Leaf" but later changed it to "Joaquin" as a tribute to his late brother River Phoenix.

ANSWERS
1. Elton John 2. Lady Gaga 3. Rihanna 4. Katy Perry 5. Bruno Mars 6. Bob Dylan 7. Jay-Z 8. Bono 9. Jamie Foxx 10. Lil Wayne 11. Ringo Starr 12. Shania Twain 13. Marilyn Monroe 14. Snoop Dogg 15. Alice Cooper

CELEBRITY BUSINESSES

ROUND RULES: In this round, the question will be the name of a business. The answer is the celebrity that started the business.

1. — The Honest Company - Beauty, baby, and cleaning products

2. — Good American - Women's clothing

3. — Fabletics - Athletic clothing

4. — Hello Sunshine - Media company

5. — Goop - "A modern lifestyle brand"

6. — Aviation Gin

7. — Virginia Black Whiskey

8. — Mansinthe - Absinthe

9. — Vital Proteins - Collagen supplements

10.— Teremana - Tequila

11.— Kinderfarms - A line of pain management products for teething children

12.— Betty Buzz - Sparking soda

13.— Avaline - Organic wine

14.— Once Upon a Farm - Clean baby food & kids' snacks

15.— Rare Beauty - Cruelty free cosmetics

DID YOU KNOW ...

Many people know Paul Newman as a legendary actor, but he also founded Newman's Own, a food company that started with salad dressing. What's lesser-known is that all of the company's profits, after taxes, were donated to charity. Since its inception in 1982, Newman's Own has donated over $550 million to various charitable organizations.

ANSWERS
1. Jessica Alba 2. Khloe Kardashian 3. Kate Hudson 4. Reese Witherspoon 5. Gwyneth Paltrow 6. Ryan Reynolds 7. Drake 8. Marilyn Manson 9. Jennifer Aniston 10. Dwayne Johnson 11. Jessica Beil 12. Blake Lively 13. Cameron Diaz 14. Jennifer Garner 15. Selena Gomez

CATCH PHRASES

ROUND RULES: In this round, the question will be a catchphrase. The answer will be the person or character that is known for the phrase.

1. — "Make it so"

2. — "That's hot"

3. — "Wubba-lubba-dub-dub!"

4. — "Just keep swimming"

5. — "That's so fetch!"

6. — "Alright, alright, alright"

7. — "Bazinga!"

8. — "Eat My Shorts"

9. — "Did I Do That?"

10. — "The tribe has spoken"

11. — "Yabba dabba doo!"

12. — "Marcia, Marcia, Marcia!"

13. — "I am not a crook"

14. — "Dy-no-mite!"

15. — "You can't see me"

DID YOU KNOW ...

Dwayne "The Rock" Johnson's catchphrase became his signature rallying cry during his WWE career. Interestingly, the phrase was inspired by his grandmother, who used to say something similar to him as a child. The Rock's electrifying delivery of the catchphrase contributed to his immense popularity both in and out of the wrestling ring.

ANSWERS
1. Captain Jean-Luc Picard in "Star Trek: The Next Generation" 2. Paris Hilton
3. Rick Sanchez in "Rick and Morty" 4. Dory in "Finding Nemo" 5. Gretchen Wieners in "Mean Girls"
6. Matthew McConaughey / David Wooderson 7. Sheldon - Big Bang Theory 8. Bart Simpson
9. Steve Urkel 10. Jeff Probst - Survivor 11. Fred Flinstone 12. Jan, The Brady Bunch 13. Richard Nixon
14. J.J. Walker - Good Times 15. John Cena

VIDEO GAMES

1. — What is the name of the artificial intelligence in the "Halo" series?

2. — What is the name of the final boss in the classic game "The Legend of Zelda"?

3. — Which game features a character named Kratos, known for his use of the Blades of Chaos?

4. — What is the name of the planet that The Elder Scrolls series takes place in?

5. — What is the name of the orange ghost enemy in "Pac-Man"?

6. — What does MOBA stand for?

7. — What is the maximum number of players in a standard game of "Among Us"?

8. — In the classic game "Sonic the Hedgehog," what is the name of Sonic's sidekick?

9. — In "Starcraft," what are the names of the three factions?

10.— What is the name of the island setting in the classic game "The Secret of Monkey Island"?

11.— What is the name of the research facility in the game "Half-Life" that is responsible for the events in the game?

12.— Which game is set in the fictional city of Rapture and features genetic modifications?

13.— Which game franchise allows players to control a character named Nathan Drake?

14.— Which game features a group of characters known as the Vault Hunters seeking treasures on the planet Pandora?

15.— In "Final Fantasy VII," what is the name of the main antagonist who seeks to summon a meteor to destroy the planet?

DID YOU KNOW ...

The iconic character Mario from the Super Mario series was named after the landlord of Nintendo's first warehouse in the United States. The landlord, Mario Segale, confronted the company about unpaid rent, and Nintendo named their character in his honor.

COMIC BOOKS

1. — Which Marvel superhero is known as the "The Devil of Hell's Kitchen"?

2. — Who is the creator of the comic book character Hellboy?

3. — What is the name of the cosmic entity that grants the Silver Surfer his powers in Marvel Comics?

4. — In DC Comics, who is the arch-nemesis of Green Arrow and is known for his expert archery skills?

5. — Frank Castle is the civilian name of what antihero?

6. — In the Fantastic Four, what is the name of Reed Richards' stretchable superhero alter ego?

7. — What is the name of Wonder Woman's home island in DC Comics?

8. — In Marvel Comics, what metal is bonded to Wolverine's skeleton to make him virtually indestructible?

9. — In the Batman comics, who is the daughter of Ra's al Ghul and a skilled assassin?

10.— Which DC Comics character is known as the "King of Atlantis"?

11.— In DC Comics, what is the civilian name of the hero known as Shazam?

12.— Who is often referred to as the "King of Comics" for his prolific contributions to the medium, including creating iconic characters like Spider-Man, the X-Men, and the Fantastic Four?

13.— In the Spider-Man comics, who is the editor-in-chief of the Daily Bugle and a frequent critic of Spider-Man?

14.— In Marvel Comics, who is the mutant with the ability to control and manipulate magnetic fields?

15.— In DC Comics, what is the real name of the superhero known as The Atom?

DID YOU KNOW ...

Wonder Woman, one of the most iconic superheroes, was created by psychologist and writer William Moulton Marston. He also invented the systolic blood pressure test, which contributed to the development of the polygraph or lie detector. Marston's wife, Elizabeth, and their partner Olive Byrne inspired the character's creation.

ANSWERS
1. Daredevil 2. Mike Mignola 3. Galactus 4. Merlyn/Dark Archer 5. The Punisher 6. Mr. Fantastic 7. Themyscira 8. Adamantium 9. Talia al Ghul 10. Aquaman 11. Billy Batson 12. Stan Lee 13. J. Jonah Jameson 14. Magneto 15. Ray Palmer

FICTIONAL PLACES

1. — This space station is located in the Alpha Quadrant at the mouth of the Bajoran wormhole

2. — A city, located in the center of Oz, known for its green tint

3. — This mysterious and magical land is accessed through a wardrobe and is home to talking animals, mythical creatures, and the White Witch

4. — A lush and bioluminescent moon located in the Alpha Centauri star system

5. — You can get here by tapping a brick in the wall behind the Leaky Cauldron in a specific pattern

6. — The force is strong on this desert planet

7. — This city, known for its canals and the House of Black and White, is located in the Free Cities across the Narrow Sea

8. — Prehistoric home to Fred & Barney

9. — A black, volcanic plain to the east of Gondor

10.— Which city serves as the primary setting for the outbreak of the T-virus, leading to a zombie outbreak?

11.— The gritty, dark and crime ridden metropolis where Commissioner Gordon, Bane, and Hugo Strange hang out

12.— The street address for Homer, Marge, Bart, Lisa, and Maggie

13.— Where King Arthur held court

14.— Fast-food restaurant owned by Gustavo Fring that serves as a front for his drug empire

15.— In this place you can find The Master Sword, the Triforce, and the Ocarina of Time

DID YOU KNOW ...

Neverland, the magical island from J.M. Barrie's "Peter Pan," has its roots in earlier works. Barrie was inspired by the fictional realm of "Erewhon" (an anagram for "nowhere") in Samuel Butler's novel "Erewhon," and he incorporated elements from Scottish folklore and mythology to create the timeless world of Neverland.

ANSWERS
1. Deep Space 9 2. Emerald City 3. Narnia 4. Pandora (Avatar) 5. Diagon Alley (Harry Potter)
6. Tatooine (Star Wars) 7. Braavos (Game of Thrones) 8. Bedrock (The Flintstones)
9. Mordor (The Lord of the Rings) 10. Racoon City (Resident Evil) 11. Gotham City (Batman)
12. 742 Evergreen Terrace (The Simpsons) 13. Camelot 14. Los Pollos Hermanos 15. Hyrule (Zelda)

MUSICALS

1. ___ In which musical does the character Jean Valjean appear?

2. ___ What musical features the song "Memory" sung by the character Grizabella?

3. ___ What musical tells the story of a group of Bohemians in New York's East Village and features songs like "Seasons of Love"?

4. ___ In which musical do the characters Emcee, Sally Bowles, and Cliff Bradshaw appear?

5. ___ Which musical explores the rivalry between two silent film stars, Norma Desmond and Joe Gillis?

6. ___ In "Wicked," who is Elphaba's roommate at Shiz University?

7. ___ What musical follows the story of Tevye, a poor Jewish milkman, and his five daughters?

8. ___ In "Mamma Mia!" which Greek island is the story set on?

9. ___ What musical tells the story of a barber seeking revenge for wrongs done to him and his family?

10.— Which musical is based on the novel "Pygmalion" by George Bernard Shaw?

11.— In "The Sound of Music," what is the name of the family's governess?

12.— In "Chicago," what is the name of the protagonist who becomes a media sensation after murdering her lover?

13.— What musical tells the story of a young woman named Tracy Turnblad who dreams of dancing on a local TV show in 1960s Baltimore?

14.— In which year did "The Lion King" musical make its Broadway debut?

15.— In "The Book of Mormon," which African country are the young Mormon missionaries sent to?

DID YOU KNOW ...

- The musical "Ain't Misbehavin'" holds the record for the most costume changes in a Broadway show. The performers change costumes 36 times during the course of the production.

- The musical "Carrie," based on Stephen King's novel, had a notoriously short run on Broadway in 1988, closing after only five performances.

ANSWERS
1. Les Misérables 2. Cats 3. Rent 4. Cabaret 5. Sunset Boulevard 6. Glinda (Galinda)
7. Fiddler on the Roof 8. Kalokairi 9. Sweeney Todd 10. My Fair Lady 11. Maria 12. Roxie Hart
13. Hairspray 14. 1997 15. Uganda

11

LANGUAGE
&
LINGUISTICS

'i' BEFORE 'e', EXCEPT AFTER 'c'

ROUND RULES: In this round, the questions describes or defines a word that breaks the english grammar rule of " 'i' before 'e' except after 'c' ". The answer is the word that breaks the rule.

1. — Belonging to the very distant past and no longer in existence

2. — A pale sandy yellowish-brown color

3. — An inner feeling or voice viewed as acting as a guide to the rightness or wrongness of one's behavior

4. — The creator and/or a supreme being

5. — Lose or be deprived of (property or a right or privilege) as a penalty for wrongdoing

6. — An optical instrument that uses mirrors to create symmetrical patterns

7. — Not the one nor the other of two people or things

8. — To take or lay hold suddenly or forcibly

9. — Something is striking odd or unusual, especially in an unsettling way

10. — Of enormous proportions or effect

11. — A person living near or next door to the speaker or person referred to

12. — Cause (someone) to believe something that is not true, typically in order to gain some personal advantage

13. — Use of free time for enjoyment

14. — A group of living organisms consisting of similar individuals capable of exchanging genes or interbreeding

15. — A piece of fine material worn by women to protect or conceal the face

DID YOU KNOW ...

The rule is a simplification and may not account for every word in the English language. There are actually more words that do not adhere to the rule than words that do.

ANSWERS
1. Ancient 2. Beige 3. Conscience 4. Deity 5.Forfeit 6. Kaleidoscope 7. Neither 8. Seize 9. Weird
10. Seismic 11. Neighbor 12. Deceive 13. Leisure 14. Species 15. Veil

GRAB BAG

1. ___ What idiom comes from the Latin phrase "cum grano salis"

2. ___ English editions of Scrabble have one letter that is worth five points. What is it?

3. ___ Which term, integral to graphic design, denotes the "art and technique of arranging type to make written language legible, readable, and appealing"?

4. ___ What is the name of the annual national spelling competition held in the United States?

5. ___ Name the missing romance language: Spanish, French, Italian, Romanian, and ___________.

6. ___ In the "Star Wars" universe, what language is primarily spoken by Wookiees, including Chewbacca?

7. ___ What word stems from the Roman practice of punishing military units by executing one in every ten soldiers and comes from the Latin word "decimare," which means "to tithe" or "to take a tenth."

8. ___ The slang term "bae" is an acronym. What does it stand for?

9. ___ What latin phrase translates to "seize the day" in English?

10.— What is the longest word in NATO phonetic alphabet?

11.— In George Orwell's novel "1984," what is the controlled language created by the totalitarian state as a tool to limit freedom of thought and concepts deemed subversive?

12.— What is the only letter in the English alphabet with more than one syllable when pronounced?

13.— What word comes from the Italian word "quaranta giorni," meaning "forty days"? It originally referred to the practice of isolating ships and their crews for a period of forty days to prevent the spread of disease

14.— What fictional language is used by the Minions in the "Despicable Me" film series?

15.— Somnambulating is a fancy term for what nighttime activity?

DID YOU KNOW ...

Contrary to popular belief, this phrase "saved by the bell" has nothing to do with boxing. It originated in the 19th century and refers to being saved from being buried alive by the invention of the safety coffin with a bell attached.

ANSWERS
1. Take with a grain of salt 2. 'K' 3. Typography 4. The Scripps National Spelling Bee 5. Portuguese
6. Shyriiwook 7. Decimate 8. Before anything else 9. Carpe diem 10. November 11. Newspeak
12."W" 13. Quarantine 14. Minionese 15. Sleepwalking

WORD ORIGINS

1. — What word comes from the Greek words "etumon," meaning "true," and "logos," meaning "word" or "study"?

2. — This word comes from an Italian word meaning "soft-loud," reflecting the instrument's ability to produce both soft and loud sounds

3. — From which language does the word "pyramid" originate?

4. — This word comes from the combination of two japanese words meaning "harbor," and "wave"

5. — "This word comes from the Persian word meaning "leg garment"

6. — This word represents good luck in finding things unintentionally and comes from a Persian fairy tale where the characters made discoveries by chance

7. — This word comes from a Czech word "meaning "forced labor" or "drudgery"

8. — This word come from "salarium," which referred to a soldier's allowance for the purchase of salt, a valuable commodity in ancient times

9. — From which language does the word "karaoke" originate?

10.— This word comes from the French word that mean "to stereotype"

11.— From which language does the word "safari" originate?

12.— This word comes from the Hindi word "bangla," meaning "of Bengal," where one-story houses were common

13.— This word comes from the Hokkien Chinese word referring to a sauce made from fermented fish

14.— This word comes from the Old Norse word "afugr" which means "turned the wrong way" or "crooked"

15.— What word did the phrase "Light Amplification by Stimulated Emission of Radiation" create?

DID YOU KNOW ...

"Karaoke" comes from the Japanese words "kara," meaning "empty," and "okesutora," meaning "orchestra."

ANSWERS
1. Etymology 2. Piano (pianoforte) 3. Greek 4. Tsunami 5. Pajamas 6. Serendipity 7. Robot (robota)
8. Salary 9. Japanese 10. Cliché 11. Swahili 12. Bungalow 13. Ketchup 14. Awkward 15. Laser

GRAB BAG 2

1. — What is the study of the structure and form of words called?

2. — Which ancient writing system used wedge-shaped symbols and was commonly used in Mesopotamia?

3. — In linguistics, what does the acronym ESL stand for?

4. — What is the term for a word or phrase that is spelled the same backward as forward?

5. — What is the last letter of the Greek alphabet?

6. — What is the most widely spoken language in Africa?

7. — What is the official language of Brazil?

8. — What word comes from the Greek word "dis," meaning "bad," and "astron," meaning "star." It originally referred to an event blamed on the position of the stars, such as an ill-fated astrological event

9. — In Morse code, which letter is represented by a single dot?

10.— What is the term for a sentence that gives a command or makes a request?

11.— What is the longest English word that can be written using only one row of a standard QWERTY keyboard?

12.— What is the only English word that begins and ends with "und"?

13.— In the NATO phonetic alphabet, what word represents the letter "V"?

14.— In Braille, how many dots are used to represent each letter?

15.— What is the term for words that imitate the sounds they describe, like "buzz" or "hiss"?

DID YOU KNOW ...

The word "sincere" has an interesting origin related to authenticity. It comes from the Latin words "sine" (without) and "cera" (wax). In ancient Rome, sculptors would use wax to fill in imperfections in their work. A sculpture described as "sine cera" (without wax) indicated that it was genuine and not hiding flaws.

ANSWERS
1. Morphology 2. Cuneiform 3. English as a Second Language 4. Palindrome 5. Omega 6. Swahili
7. Portuguese 8. Disaster 9. E 10. Imperative sentence 11. Typewriter 12. Underground 13. Victor
14. Six 15. Onomatopoeia

WHAT'S THE WORD FOR...

1. — What is a duel between three people called?

2. — What do you call the dot above the letters "i" and "j"?

3. — What is the term for the fear of running out of reading material?

4. — What is the term for the indentation at the bottom of a wine bottle?

5. — What do you call the space between your eyebrows?

6. — What is the term for the fear of heights?

7. — What is the word for the part of a book that lists keywords and directs you to the pages where they appear?

8. — What is the word for the study of handwriting?

9. — What is the term for the fear of making decisions?

10.— What is the word for a sentence that contains every letter of the alphabet at least once?

11.— What is the term for the fear of being without mobile phone coverage?

12.— What do you call a word or phrase that is spelled by rearranging the letters of another word or phrase?

13.— What do you call the irrational fear that somewhere, somehow, a duck is watching you?

14.— What do you call a word that is spelled incorrectly but sounds the same as the correct one?

15.— What is the term for the small, pointed metal or plastic piece at the end of a shoelace?

DID YOU KNOW ...

The sentence "A man, a plan, a canal, Panama!" is a palindrome, meaning it reads the same backward as forward. It was created as a mnemonic to remember the construction of the Panama Canal.

ANSWERS
1.Truel or Triel **2.** Tittle **3**. Abibliophobia **4.** Punt **5.** Glabella **6.** Acrophobia **7.** Index **8**. Graphology
9. Decidophobia **10.** Pangram **11**. Nomophobia **12.** Anagram **13.** Anatidaephobia **14.**Homophones
15. Aglet

GRAB BAG 3

1. — Which language is known for having the most native speakers worldwide?

2. — What is the world's oldest known written language, dating back to ancient Mesopotamia?

3. — What is the only letter that doesn't appear in the periodic table of elements?

4. — Which Indo-Aryan language is the official language of Bangladesh and has over 300 million native speakers?

5. — In which country is Tagalog an official language?

6. — What word comes directly from "alpha", and "beta", the first two letters of the Greek alphabet?

7. — Which English word is spelled the same forwards, backwards, upside down, and right side up?

8. — Who is known for creating the first comprehensive dictionary of the English language, titled "A Dictionary of the English Language," in the 18th century?

9. — Which is the only country where Latin is the official language?

10.— What does the acronym "AARP" represent in the United States?

11.— What is the only English word that ends in "-mt"?

12.— What is the term for the smallest unit of sound in a language that can change the meaning of a word?

13.— In the English alphabet, which letter is the only one not to appear in any U.S. state name?

14.— What does the acronym "GPS" stand for in navigation technology?

15.— What is the only word in the english language that has 3 consecutive double letters?

DID YOU KNOW ...

Rotokas, spoken in Papua New Guinea, has one of the smallest consonant inventories of any language. It has only six consonants: /p, t, k, b, d, g/. Despite its limited consonants, it has a relatively large vowel inventory.

ANSWERS
1. Mandarin Chinese 2. Sumerian 3. J 4. Bengali 5. The Philippines 6. Alphabet 7. Swims
8. Samuel Johnson 9. Vatican City 10. American Association of Retired Persons 11.Dreamt 12. Phoneme
13. Q 14. Global Positioning System 15. Bookkeeper

ACRONYMS

ROUND RULES: In this round the question lists an acronym. The answer is the full version of the words the acronym represents.

1. — SCUBA

2. — NASA

3. — NATO

4. — SWAT

5. — GIF

6. — RSVP

7. — JPEG

8. — DVD

9. — AM/PM

10. — IQ

11. — POTUS

12. — OSHA

13. — CAPTCHA

14. — NASDAQ

15. — MADD

DID YOU KNOW ...

A Taser is an electroshock weapon used for incapacitating targets. The term "Taser" is actually an acronym for "Thomas A. Swift's Electric Rifle," named after a fictional character in a book series.

ANSWERS
1. Self-Contained Underwater Breathing Apparatus 2. National Aeronautics and Space Administration
3. North Atlantic Treaty Organization 4. Special Weapons And Tactics 5. Graphics Interchange Format
6. Répondez s'il vous plaît (French for "Please respond") 7. Joint Photographic Experts Group
8. Digital Versatile Disc 9. Ante meridiem and post meridiem 10. Intelligence Quotient
11. President of the United States 12. Occupational Safety and Health Administration
13. Completely Automated Public Turing test to tell Computers and Humans Apart
14. National Association of Securities Dealers Automated Quotations 15. Mothers Against Drunk Driving

12

GENERAL KNOWLEDGE

HOLIDAYS

1. — In which country did the tradition of exchanging Christmas gifts originate?

2. — What holiday is known as the "Festival of Lights"?

3. — What is the name of the traditional Scottish New Year's celebration?

4. — In what country did the tradition of Easter egg rolling originate?

5. — The Irish holiday Oíche Shamhna is celebrated as what holiday in the United States?

6. — What is the official flower of Mother's Day?

7. — In what month is Canada Day celebrated?

8. — Which country is credited with the tradition of the Christmas tree?

9. — In the United States, which president officially established Thanksgiving as a national holiday?

10.— On what day is Boxing Day traditionally celebrated in Great Britain, Australia, Canada, and New Zealand?

11.— What Hindu festival is also known as the "Festival of Colors"?

12.— In Sweden, what holiday marks the official start of the Christmas season?

13.— What is the name of the Jewish New Year?

14.— What holiday is celebrated on February 2nd, marking the midpoint between the winter solstice and the spring equinox?

15.— Which May holiday celebrates the Mexican victory over the French Empire at the Battle of Puebla in 1862?

DID YOU KNOW ...

In Austria, there's a tradition known as Krampusnacht (Krampus Night) on December 5th. Krampus, a demonic figure with horns and a long tongue, is said to accompany St. Nicholas, punishing naughty children while St. Nicholas rewards the well-behaved.

ANSWERS
1. Ancient Rome 2. Hanukkah 3. Hogmanay 4.United Kingdom 5. Halloween 6. Carnation 7. July
8. Germany 9. Abraham Lincoln 10. December 26 11. Holi 12. St. Lucia Day 13. Rosh Hashanah
14. Groundhog Day 15. Cinco de Mayo

WHAT COMES NEXT?

1. — PLANETS: Mercury, Venus, Earth, Mars, _______

2. — STAGES OF MITOSIS: Prophase, Metaphase, _______

3. — DAYS OF CHRISTMAS: twelve drummers drumming, eleven pipers piping, ten lords a-leaping, nine ladies dancing, ___________

4. — PRIME NUMBERS: 2,3,5,7,11,13,17,19,23, ____

5. — PERIODIC ELEMENTS: Helium, Lithium, Beryllium, Boron, Carbon, Nitrogen, _______

6. — COLORS OF THE RAINBOW: Red, Orange, Yellow, Green, _____

7. — HARRY POTTER BOOKS: Sorcerer's Stone, Chamber of Secrets, Prisoner of Azkaban, Goblet of Fire, _________

8. — GREEK ALPHABET: Alpha, Beta, Gamma, Delta, Epsilon, Zeta, Eta, ________

9. — PHASES OF THE MOON: New Moon, Waxing Crescent, First Quarter, Waxing Gibbous, ________

10. — STAR WARS EPISODES: The Phantom Menace, Attack of the Clones, Revenge of Sith, A New Hope, ________

11. — TAXONOMIC SYSTEM: Species, Genus, Family, ________

12. — GENERATIONS: Greatest Generation, Silent Generation, Baby Boomers, ________

13. — US PRESIDENTS: Andrew Jackson, Martin Van Buren, William Henry Harrison, ________

14. — ROMAN NUMERALS: XLII, XLIII, XLIV, ________

15. — ASTROLOGICAL SIGNS: Aries, Taurus, Gemini, ________

DID YOU KNOW ...

The names of the days of the week in English are derived from Norse mythology. For example, Thursday comes from Thor's day, Friday from Frigg's day, and Wednesday from Woden's (Odin's) day. In many languages, the days of the week are named after celestial bodies or gods from various mythologies. For instance, in Spanish, Monday is "lunes" (from "Luna" meaning Moon), and Sunday is "domingo" (from "Dominus" meaning Lord).

ANSWERS
1. Jupiter 2. Anaphase 3. Eight maids a-milking 4. 29 5. Oxygen 6. Blue 7. Order of the Phoenix
8. Theta 9. Full Moon 10. The Empire Strikes Back 11. Order 12. Generation X 13. John Tyler
14. XLV 15. Cancer

TECHNOLOGY

1. — In computer programming, what does the acronym "HTML" stand for?

2. — What is the programming language developed by Apple for iOS and macOS app development?

3. — What is the unit of measurement for computer memory and storage equal to 1024 bytes?

4. — Which company developed the first commercially available computer mouse?

5. — What does the term "Wi-Fi" stand for in wireless networking?

6. — Which programming language was created by James Gosling and Mike Sheridan at Sun Microsystems and is known for its slogan "Write Once, Run Anywhere"?

7. — Which technology is used to identify and authenticate users based on their unique physical or behavioral traits?

8. — In computer graphics, what does the acronym "RGB" stand for?

9. — In computer networking, what is the name of the unique address assigned to each device connected to a network?

10.— What programming language, created by Guido van Rossum, is known for its readability and is often used for web development and artificial intelligence?

11.— In computer science, what does the acronym "URL" stand for?

12.— In networking, what does the acronym "LAN" stand for?

13.— What is the term for a type of malicious software that encrypts a user's files and demands payment for their release?

14.— In computer networking, what does the acronym "VPN" stand for?

15.— In telecommunications, what does the acronym "VoIP" stand for?

DID YOU KNOW ...

Researchers are exploring the possibility of using DNA as a medium for data storage. DNA can store immense amounts of information in a compact form. In 2019, scientists encoded a full computer operating system, a movie, and other files into strands of DNA.

ANSWERS
1. HyperText Markup Language 2. Swift 3. Kilobyte (KB). 4. Xerox 5. Wireless Fidelity 6. Java
7. Biometrics 8. Red, Green, Blue 9. IP Address (Internet Protocol Address) 10. Python
11.Uniform Resource Locator 12. Local Area Network 13. Ransomware 14. Virtual Private Network
15. Voice over Internet Protocol

MATH

1. — What is the sum of the first 100 positive integers?

2. — If a right-angled triangle has legs of length 3 and 4, what is the length of the hypotenuse?

3. — In a geometric sequence, what is the common ratio if the terms are 2, 4, 8, 16, ...?

4. — If a square has a side length of 6 units, what is its perimeter?

5. — What is the sum of the interior angles of a hexagon?

6. — Solve for x: $3x-7=14$

7. — If a rectangle has a length of 8 units and a width of 5 units, what is its area?

8. — Jane ordered 8 pizzas for a party. Each pizza was cut into 6 slices. If there were 24 people at the party, how many slices of pizza does each person get?

9. — If a regular pentagon has a side length of 12 units, what is its perimeter?

10. — A store is having a 30% off sale on all items. If a shirt originally costs $40, how much will it cost after the discount?

11. — If a triangle has a base of 10 inches and a height of 8 inches, what is the area of the triangle?

12. — Solve for y: 2y+5=17

13. — In trigonometry, what is the reciprocal of the sine function?

14. — If a regular octahedron has 88 faces, how many vertices does it have?

15. — A train travels at a speed of 60 miles per hour. If the train travels for 3 hours, how far does it go?

DID YOU KNOW ...

The Banach-Tarski Paradox is a counterintuitive result in set-theoretic geometry. It states that a solid sphere can be decomposed into a finite number of non-overlapping pieces, and, using only rotations and translations, these pieces can be rearranged to form two identical solid spheres of the same size as the original.

ANSWERS
1. 5050 2. 5 3. 2 4. 24 units 5. 720 degrees 6. x=7 7. 40 square units 8. 2 slices 9. 60 units 10. $28
11. 40 square inches 12. y=6 13. Cosecant 14. 6 15. 180 miles

BOARD GAMES

1. — In chess, what is the only piece that can jump over other pieces?

2. — In this game, players use train cards to claim railway routes connecting cities. What is the game called?

3. — Which cooperative board game tasks players with curing diseases and preventing global outbreaks?

4. — How much money do players receive at the beginning of a standard game of Monopoly?

5. — What classic game involves players drawing cards with categories and trying to come up with items that fit the categories within a time limit?

6. — What game challenges players to guess the identity of a hidden character by asking yes/no questions?

7. — In the game of Clue (or Cluedo), how many rooms are there in the mansion?

8. — How many squares are on a standard chessboard?

9. — In this deduction game, players use logic and deduction to uncover the hidden colors of their opponents' secret code. What is the game called?

10.— In Settlers of Catan, what 5 resources can players collect and trade to build settlements and cities?

11.— In Risk, what is the continent that provides the highest reinforcement bonus for controlling all its territories?

12.— What classic strategy game involves capturing your opponent's flag while defending your own?

13.— How many cards is a player dealt in a standard hand of cribbage?

14.— In Scrabble, how many points are indicated on the tile for the letter "F"?

15.— In what board game do you pop a clear dome in the center of the board in order to roll the die?

DID YOU KNOW ...

Senet, an ancient Egyptian board game, dates back to around 3500 BCE, making it one of the oldest known board games. It was played on a grid of 30 squares arranged in three rows of ten and involved strategy, luck, and symbolic significance, often associated with the afterlife.

ANSWERS
1. The Knight 2. Ticket to Ride 3. Pandemic 4. $1,500 5. Scattergories 6. Guess Who? 7. 9 8. 64
9. Mastermind 10. Brick, grain, lumber, ore, and wool 11. Asia 12. Stratego 13. 6 14. 4 15. Trouble

CLASSIC CARS

1. — In what year was the Ford Mustang first introduced?

2. — What classic car model was famously driven by James Bond in several films, including "Goldfinger"?

3. — What classic car brand is famous for its luxury vehicles, including models like the Silver Ghost and Phantom?

4. — In what year did the Volkswagen Beetle make its debut?

5. — What was the first mass-produced car model by the Ford Motor Company, introduced in 1908?

6. — In what year was the first Chevrolet Corvette introduced?

7. — What classic car brand, known for its sports cars, was founded in England in 1935 by Sir William Lyons?

8. — What classic car, produced by Jaguar from 1961 to 1975, is renowned for its sleek design and high-performance capabilities?

9. — Which classic Italian sports car manufacturer is known for models like the Miura and Countach?

10.— In what year did Chevrolet introduce the first-generation Camaro?

11.— In what year was the first-generation Ford Bronco introduced as a compact SUV?

12.— Which classic car brand produced the iconic "GTO Judge" model?

13.— What classic American muscle car, introduced by Dodge in 1966, is famous for its powerful Hemi engine?

14.— Which classic car, introduced by Porsche in 1963, is renowned for its rear-engine design and distinctive round headlights?

15.— Which classic car brand produced the Road Runner model?

DID YOU KNOW ...

The iconic hood ornament of Rolls-Royce cars, known as the Spirit of Ecstasy, is often colloquially referred to as the "Flying Lady" or the "Silver Lady." Designed by sculptor Charles Robinson Sykes, the ornament has adorned Rolls-Royce vehicles since 1911.

ANSWERS
1. 1964 2. The Aston Martin DB5 3. Rolls-Royce 4. 1938 5. Ford Model T 6. 1953 7. Jaguar
8. E-Type (or XK-E) 9. Lamborghini 10. 1966 11. 1966 12. Pontiac 13. Dodge Charger
14. Porsche 911 15. Plymouth

ANIMALS

1. — What is a group of flamingos called?

2. — What is the largest living species of lizard?

3. — What is the name for a group of porcupines?

4. — Which marine animal is often called a "sea cow" and is known for its herbivorous diet?

5. — Which bird species is the fastest flyer, capable of reaching speeds up to 240 mph (386 km/h)?

6. — What is the term for a group of crows?

7. — What is the largest mammal on Earth?

8. — What is the scientific term for a group of owls?

9. — Which insect is the only one capable of turning its head 180 degrees?

10.— Which species of penguin is the largest and heaviest?

11.— What is the smallest mammal in the world?

12.— Which animal has the longest lifespan in the animal kingdom?

13.— What is the largest species of sea turtle?

14.— What is the world's largest species of rodent?

15.— What is a group of lions called?

DID YOU KNOW ...

The axolotl, a type of salamander, is known for its extraordinary regenerative abilities. Unlike other amphibians, axolotls can regrow not only limbs but also parts of their heart, spinal cord, and even parts of their brain.

ANSWERS
1. A Flamboyance 2. Komodo Dragon 3. Prickle 4. Manatee 5. Peregrine Falcon 6. Murder 7. Blue Whale
8. Parliament 9. Praying Mantis 10. Emperor Penguin 11. Etruscan Shrew 12. Ocean Quahog
13. Leatherback Turtle 14. Capybara 15. Pride

TRIVIA MATH

1. — The number of teams in the NFL plus the number of Canadian provinces

2. — The number of bones in the human body plus the year that the Declaration of Independence was signed

3. — The number of Senators in the US Senate divided by the number of protons in a Hydrogen atom

4. — The number of keys on a standard piano divided by the number of phases of the moon

5. — The number of elements in the periodic table minus the number of players from a team allowed on the field at one time, in baseball

6. — The number of amendments to the US Constitution plus the number of rings on the olympic flag

7. — The number of counties in the state of Texas, plus the total known number of species of fish, divided by zero

8. — The number of face cards in a standard deck of playing cards multiplied by the number of letters in the english alphabet

9. — The number of inches in a yard minus the number of timezones in the world

10.— The number of Grams in a Kilogram multiplied by the number of Pints in a Gallon

11.— The number of symphonies composed by Ludwig Van Beethoven plus the number of ounces in a pound

12.— A perfect bowling score plus the number of faces on a dodecahedron

13.— The number of feet in a mile minus the number of pairs of chromosomes in humans

14.— The smallest prime number multiplied by the number of oscars won by the film "Titanic'

15.— The number of legs on a lobster divided by the number of humps on a Bactrian Camel

DID YOU KNOW ...

The Four Color Theorem, first conjectured in the 19th century and proven in 1976, states that any map can be colored with just four colors in such a way that no two adjacent regions share the same color. This theorem is a result of graph theory, a branch of mathematics.

ANSWERS
1. 42 (32 + 10) **2.** 1982 (206 + 1776) **3.** 100 (100/1) **4.** 11 (88/8) **5.** 109 (118-9) **6.** 32 (27+5) **7.** 0
8. 312 (12x26) **9.** 12 (36-24) **10.** 8,000 (1,000 x 8) **11.** 25 (9+16) **12.** 312 (300+12) **13.** 5,257 (5,280 - 23)
14. 22 (2x11) **15.** 5 (10/2)

SCORING

SCORING

LITERATURE

1. NAME THE WORK: _______
2. NAME THE STORY: _______
3. NAME THE AUTHOR: _______
4. GRAB BAG: _______
5. CHILDREN'S STORIES: _______
6. GRAB BAG 2: _______
7. 21st CENTURY AUTHORS: _______

MUSIC

1. GRAB BAG: _______
2. NAME THE ARTIST: _______
3. NAME THE ARTIST 2: _______
4. GRAB BAG 2: _______
5. MUSICAL ACHIEVEMENTS: _______
6. MOVIE MUSIC: _______
7. FIRST #1 ON BILLBOARD: _______

SPORTS

1. ACHIEVEMENTS: _______
2. NAME THE ATHLETE: _______
3. COLLEGE SPORTS: _______
4. GRAB BAG: _______
5. GRAB BAG 2: _______
6. GRAB BAG 3: _______
7. GRAB BAG 4: _______

GEOGRAPHY

1. WORLD CAPITOLS: _______
2. WATER: _______
3. NAME THE COUNTRY: _______
4. GRAB BAG: _______
5. GRAB BAG 2: _______
6. GRAB BAG 3: _______
7. GRAB BAG 4: _______

MOVIES & TV

1. MOVIE LINES: _______
2. MOVIE LINES 2: _______
3. MOVIE MONSTERS: _______
4. ACADEMY AWARDS: _______
5. TV: _______
6. TV 2: _______
7. GRAB BAG: _______

SCIENCE

1. SCIENTIFIC DISCOVERIES: _______
2. SPACE: _______
3. BIOLOGY: _______
4. GRAB BAG: _______
5. GRAB BAG 2: _______
6. GRAB BAG 3: _______
7. GRAB BAG 4: _______

SCORING

FOOD & DRINK

1. **NAME THE BRAND:** _______
2. **NAME THE FOOD:** _______
3. **MOVIE & TV FOOD:** _______
4. **GRAB BAG:** _______
5. **ALCOHOL YOU LATER:** _______
6. **GRAB BAG 2:** _______
7. **GRAB BAG 3:** _______

POP CULTURE

1. **STAGE NAMES:** _______
2. **CELEBRITY BUSINESSES:** _______
3. **CATCH PHRASES:** _______
4. **VIDEO GAMES:** _______
5. **COMIC BOOKS:** _______
6. **FICTIONAL PLACES:** _______
7. **MUSICALS:** _______

MYTHOLOGY & FOLKLORE

1. **GREEK MYTHOLOGY:** _______
2. **NORSE MYTHOLOGY:** _______
3. **ROMAN MYTHOLOGY:** _______
4. **MYTHICAL CREATURES:** _______
5. **FOLKLORE:** _______
6. **GRAB BAG:** _______
7. **GRAB BAG 2:** _______

LANUAGE & LINGUISTICS

1. **EXCEPT AFTER 'c":** _______
2. **GRAB BAG:** _______
3. **WORD ORIGINS:** _______
4. **GRAB BAG 2:** _______
5. **WHAT'S THE WORD FOR:** _______
6. **GRAB BAG 3:** _______
7. **ACRONYMS:** _______

HISTORY

1. **WORLD WAR I:** _______
2. **WORLD WAR II:** _______
3. **RECENT HISTORY:** _______
4. **ANCIENT CIVILIZATIONS:** _______
5. **RULERS:** _______
6. **GRAB BAG:** _______
7. **NAME THE YEAR:** _______

GENERAL KNOWLEDGE

1. **HOLIDAYS:** _______
2. **WHAT COMES NEXT:** _______
3. **TECHNOLOGY:** _______
4. **MATH:** _______
5. **BOARD GAMES:** _______
6. **CLASSIC CARS:** _______
7. **ANIMALS:** _______
8. **TRIVIA MATH:** _______

THE END.